Endangered
OCEANS

Opposing Viewpoints®

Other Books of Related Interest

Endangered
OCEANS

Opposing Viewpoints®

Louise I. Gerdes, *Book Editor*

Daniel Leone, *President*
Bonnie Szumski, *Publisher*
Scott Barbour, *Managing Editor*
Helen Cothran, *Senior Editor*

OPPOSING
VIEWPOINTS®
SERIES

GREENHAVEN
PRESS®

THOMSON
GALE

San Diego • Detroit • New York • San Francisco • Cleveland
New Haven, Conn. • Waterville, Maine • London • Munich

LIBRARY OF CONGRESS CATALOGING-IN-PUBLICATION DATA

Endangered oceans : opposing viewpoints / Louise I. Gerdes, book editor.
    p. cm. — (Opposing viewpoints series)
Includes bibliographical references and index.
ISBN 0-7377-2275-4 (pbk. : alk. paper) — ISBN 0-7377-2274-6 (lib. : alk. paper)
    1. Marine resources conservation. 2. Marine pollution. 3. Ocean—Environmental aspects. I. Gerdes, Louise I. II. Opposing viewpoints series (Unnumbered)
GC1018.E53 2004
333.95'616—dc21   2003054015

Printed in the United States of America

"Congress shall make
no law. . . abridging the
freedom of speech, or of
the press."

First Amendment to the U.S. Constitution

The basic foundation of our democracy is the First
Amendment guarantee of freedom of expression.
The Opposing Viewpoints Series is dedicated to the
concept of this basic freedom and the idea that it is
more important to practice it than to enshrine it.

Contents

Why Consider Opposing Viewpoints?

"The only way in which a human being can make some approach to knowing the whole of a subject is by hearing what can be said about it by persons of every variety of opinion and studying all modes in which it can be looked at by every character of mind. No wise man ever acquired his wisdom in any mode but this."

John Stuart Mill

In our media-intensive culture it is not difficult to find differing opinions. Thousands of newspapers and magazines and dozens of radio and television talk shows resound with differing points of view. The difficulty lies in deciding which opinion to agree with and which "experts" seem the most credible. The more inundated we become with differing opinions and claims, the more essential it is to hone critical reading and thinking skills to evaluate these ideas. Opposing Viewpoints books address this problem directly by presenting stimulating debates that can be used to enhance and teach these skills. The varied opinions contained in each book examine many different aspects of a single issue. While examining these conveniently edited opposing views, readers can develop critical thinking skills such as the ability to compare and contrast authors' credibility, facts, argumentation styles, use of persuasive techniques, and other stylistic tools. In short, the Opposing Viewpoints Series is an ideal way to attain the higher-level thinking and reading skills so essential in a culture of diverse and contradictory opinions.

In addition to providing a tool for critical thinking, Opposing Viewpoints books challenge readers to question their own strongly held opinions and assumptions. Most people form their opinions on the basis of upbringing, peer pressure, and personal, cultural, or professional bias. By reading carefully balanced opposing views, readers must directly confront new ideas as well as the opinions of those with whom they disagree. This is not to simplistically argue that everyone who reads opposing views will—or should—change his or her opinion. Instead, the series enhances readers' understanding of their own views by encouraging confrontation with opposing ideas. Careful examination of others' views can lead to the readers' understanding of the logical inconsistencies in their own opinions, perspective on why they hold an opinion, and the consideration of the possibility that their opinion requires further evaluation.

Evaluating Other Opinions

To ensure that this type of examination occurs, Opposing Viewpoints books present all types of opinions. Prominent spokespeople on different sides of each issue as well as well-known professionals from many disciplines challenge the reader. An additional goal of the series is to provide a forum for other, less known, or even unpopular viewpoints. The opinion of an ordinary person who has had to make the decision to cut off life support from a terminally ill relative, for example, may be just as valuable and provide just as much insight as a medical ethicist's professional opinion. The editors have two additional purposes in including these less known views. One, the editors encourage readers to respect others' opinions—even when not enhanced by professional credibility. It is only by reading or listening to and objectively evaluating others' ideas that one can determine whether they are worthy of consideration. Two, the inclusion of such viewpoints encourages the important critical thinking skill of objectively evaluating an author's credentials and bias. This evaluation will illuminate an author's reasons for taking a particular stance on an issue and will aid in readers' evaluation of the author's ideas.

It is our hope that these books will give readers a deeper understanding of the issues debated and an appreciation of the complexity of even seemingly simple issues when good and honest people disagree. This awareness is particularly important in a democratic society such as ours in which people enter into public debate to determine the common good. Those with whom one disagrees should not be regarded as enemies but rather as people whose views deserve careful examination and may shed light on one's own.

Thomas Jefferson once said that "difference of opinion leads to inquiry, and inquiry to truth." Jefferson, a broadly educated man, argued that "if a nation expects to be ignorant and free . . . it expects what never was and never will be." As individuals and as a nation, it is imperative that we consider the opinions of others and examine them with skill and discernment. The Opposing Viewpoints Series is intended to help readers achieve this goal.

David L. Bender and Bruno Leone,
Founders

Greenhaven Press anthologies primarily consist of previously published material taken from a variety of sources, including periodicals, books, scholarly journals, newspapers, government documents, and position papers from private and public organizations. These original sources are often edited for length and to ensure their accessibility for a young adult audience. The anthology editors also change the original titles of these works in order to clearly present the main thesis of each viewpoint and to explicitly indicate the opinion presented in the viewpoint. These alterations are made in consideration of both the reading and comprehension levels of a young adult audience. Every effort is made to ensure that Greenhaven Press accurately reflects the original intent of the authors included in this anthology.

Introduction

"Were it not for the fact that we are such visual creatures, our sense of community with the ocean should be easier and more intuitive to grasp than even our sense of the land, because our connection with the sea is more intimate. . . . We are, in a sense, soft vessels of seawater. Seventy percent of our bodies are water, the same percentage that covers Earth's surface."
—Carl Safina, marine biologist and conservationist

People do not often think about how much humans depend on the world's oceans. Oceans regulate the climate, maintain a livable atmosphere, and break down natural wastes. According to marine biologist and conservationist Carl Safina, "Without an ocean, this planet would merely spin unnamed three orbits from a star, its browned-out face its own sterile moonscape." Nevertheless, people treat the oceans as if they were inexhaustible both in terms of what they produce and in what they can absorb. Although people are now more aware of threats to the world's oceans, marine conservation efforts still comprise only a small part of total conservation efforts. For example, about 18 percent of U.S. land is protected while only 0.4 percent of U.S. waters are protected. Unlike land, which is visible and stationary, the ocean is opaque and fluid. These characteristics make marine conservation efforts more difficult than efforts to protect the land.

While people can readily observe destructive land use practices, abuse of the oceans often goes unseen. For this reason, laws and regulations to protect the oceans often come long after the damage has been done. Land degradation caused by the clear cutting of forests, for example, is obvious to those who live in the surrounding community. In contrast, the deep ocean floor is unseen by most people, so the devastation caused by bottom trawling equipment goes unnoticed. According to ocean policy analyst Hannah Gillelan, "Were trawls clearing swaths on land, as they do on the seafloor, the practice would have been severely curtailed or halted before now." The destruction of marine wildlife also goes unrecognized for the same reason. Tom Butler, editor of *Wild Earth*, writes, "How many of us have seen a living shark, bleeding from a gaping wound, dumped overboard to sink and die alone, a sacrifice to the whims of people who enjoy shark fin soup?"

Another challenge to marine conservation efforts is that unlike land, the ocean is fluid. In consequence, pollution affects oceans differently than its does land masses. Environmental policy analyst Anne Platt McGinn writes, "Once contaminants enter the sea, currents and tides may carry them far from the original source. Or they may be consumed by a species and move up the food chain, becoming more concentrated as they go. Both pollutants and species continually migrate across boundaries and interact, complicating protection efforts." Pollutants created and dispersed by one nation may have an impact on oceans and wildlife far from its borders. Persistent organic pollutants (POPs), synthetic chemicals that do not degrade easily, tend to circulate toward colder environments such as the Arctic. They accumulate in the fatty tissues of fish that are then consumed by predators at a more concentrated level and, as a result, have been implicated in a wide range of animal and human health problems. Although the problem of POPs is global, not until May 2001 did concerned nations sign the Stockholm Convention, an international treaty that aims to eliminate POPs.

Perhaps the greatest difficulty in protecting the world's oceans is that although ocean waters are used by many nations, no nation owns them. A nation has sovereignty over its lands and territorial sea, the small coastal strip adjacent to its shores, but no nation has sovereignty over the "high seas." Conserving open-ocean resources thus requires concerted international cooperation, a vastly more complicated effort than is involved in national land conservation efforts, which can generally be coordinated within one nation. Prior to the mid–twentieth century, this international cooperation was lacking; in fact, the use of ocean resources was guided by the freedom-of-the-seas principle. In 1609 Hugo Grotius argued in *Mare Liberum* (Free Sea) that no one owned the high seas because they could not be occupied in the sense that land can be occupied. The high seas, he claimed, were therefore free to all nations and subject to none.

In 1958, however, a number of factors prompted the United Nations to develop an international law to govern the oceans. Some coastal nations had unilaterally claimed different parts of the oceans as their own and conflicts between nations began to arise. In addition, ocean pollution had begun to threaten coastal regions and wildlife worldwide. In response, the United Nations held a series of conventions between 1958 and 1982 that resulted in the United Nations Convention on the Law of the Sea (UNCLOS), which went into effect in 1994 and, as of February 2002, has been ratified by 138 nations. Although the United States has not yet ratified the Convention, it has accepted it in principle. UNCLOS covers a wide range of ocean issues, including protection of the marine environment and the conservation and management of its resources. UNCLOS also approved a twelve-nautical-mile territorial limit for coastal nations and a two-hundred-nautical-mile Exclusive Economic Zone, in which the adjacent nation may control fishing rights, marine environmental protection, and scientific research. According to Jose Luis Jesus, a member of the International Tribunal for the Law of the Sea, the convention "has contributed much to bring stability and order to the oceans. The era of unilateral claims and sovereignty disputes . . . seem to be a thing of the past."

For other commentators, however, stability and order are not enough. The provisions of UNCLOS, they claim, are insufficient to protect the marine environment. According to researchers Robert J. Wilder, Mia J. Tegner, and Paul K. Dayton, "The scarce language in UNCLOS regarding the conservation of marine biodiversity is far more aspirational than operational." Treaties such as UNCLOS, they argue, operate using unsuccessful marine policies, often based on the outdated maxim, "Take as much as can be taken and pollute as much as can be polluted until a problem arises." These conservationists argue that a precautionary principle—preventing damage before it occurs—must be incorporated into conservation treaties.

For many, marine conservation efforts continue to lag behind those on land, and identifying how best to meet the challenges of conserving ocean and coastal resources remains the subject of debate. In *Opposing Viewpoints: Endangered Oceans*, other controversies surrounding the conservation of the world's oceans and coastal areas are debated in the following chapters: How Endangered Are the World's Oceans and Coastlines? What Ocean Management and Conservation Practices Should Be Pursued? What Strategies Would Best Promote Sustainable Fishing? What Impact Do Human Activities Have on Marine Mammals? The authors express diverse views about the extent of the threat to the world's oceans and debate the most effective ways to protect the marine environment.

CHAPTER 1

How Endangered Are the World's Oceans and Coastlines?

Chapter Preface

Considered one of the seven natural wonders of the world, the eighty-thousand-year-old Great Barrier Reef runs for about 1,250 miles along the northeastern coast of Australia. It is the largest structure ever created by living things. Coral reefs such as the Great Barrier Reef are home to one quarter of all marine plants and animals. In fact, coral reefs are considered the "rain forests of the sea," a source of tremendous biodiversity. Reef ecosystems support vast fisheries that people, especially in coastal nations, depend on for survival. Previously unknown compounds found in coral reefs offer hope as medicines. For example, a U.S. pharmaceutical company, Neurex, developed a potent painkiller from the poison of a reef-dwelling sea snail. Coral reefs also provide a beautiful undersea world that attracts snorkellers and divers, which in turn promotes a billion dollar tourist industry. Furthermore, reefs provide natural harbors and walls that protect coastlines against tides, storms, and hurricanes.

Although living coral reefs are the foundation of marine life and therefore a crucial support for human life, human activities threaten to destroy them. Each coral formation is comprised of a colony of hundreds of thousands of tiny organisms, called polyps, which jointly build a skeleton that forms the reef. Tiny one-celled plants called zooxanthellae, which give coral its bright colors, inhabit the outside layer of each coral polyp. When these organisms are expelled by warmer than average water or other stresses, the coral soon dies. Much of the stress placed on coral reefs is a result of human activities. Many coral reef fisheries have been overfished, and desperate people in the Philippines and Kenya have resorted to dynamiting reefs to obtain elusive fish. In other nations such as in East Asia, fishers stun the fish with cyanide, which ultimately kills the coral. Runoff of organic waste and chemical fertilizers used on land overloads reefs with nutrients. Excessive nutrients allow destructive algae to take over the reef, blotting out the sun that the coral needs to live. Clearcutting of forests and bulldozing for housing tracts creates loose dirt that is washed downstream to the reef, burying and eventually smothering coral. Uninformed or careless tourists add to the problem by crushing and breaking off fragile reef corals, and some reefs are mined for limestone and sand to build hotel beaches. In some regions bits of coral are broken off and sold as souvenirs.

As a result of these stresses, coral reefs are endangered worldwide. According to the National Oceanic and Atmospheric Association, nearly 27 percent of the world's coral reefs are already gone, and if nothing is done to change conditions, another two-thirds will be lost within the next thirty years, more than double the estimated losses predicted in 1998. Despite this gloomy forecast, some analysts believe that there is hope for the world's coral reefs because reefs are resilient and bounce back quickly when protected. In fact, according to Australian marine scientist Clive Wilkinson, many reefs have recovered. "We now understand the major causes of coral reef decline and there have also been sufficient management successes to show the way to reduce and even eliminate the human pressures that degrade coral reefs," he maintains.

While coral reefs off the coasts of the United States and Australia are recovering as a result of conservation and management efforts, coral reefs off the coasts of other nations have not. "Many coral reef countries have no national coral reef management or monitoring programs, and thus may be unaware of the extent of damage to their reefs," writes Wilkinson. To save the world's reefs, he argues, conservationists must show reluctant governments "that coral reef conservation pays dividends in the long run." Other commentators do not share Wilkinson's optimism. Even when governments have established reef conservation programs, they argue, the programs are often ineffective. According to *Mother Jones* editor Keith Hammond, "Government efforts in much of the world have been frankly pathetic: late, weak, underfunded, unenforced."

While many analysts agree that the world's coral reefs are seriously endangered, commentators continue to debate the effectiveness of conservation efforts. The authors of the viewpoints in the following chapter examine the extent to which the world's oceans and coastlines are endangered.

"Marine scientists, fishery biologists, conservationists, and oceanographers . . . agreed that the most pressing threats to ocean health are human-induced."

Human Activities Threaten the World's Oceans and Coastal Regions

Anne Platt McGinn

Human activities are destroying the oceans and coastal regions that people depend on for survival, argues Anne Platt McGinn in the following viewpoint. Fishing provides food and income for billions of people worldwide, she maintains, but wasteful fishing techniques have depleted key fish in the food web, threatening the entire marine ecosystem. Moreover, McGinn claims, people continue to flock to coastal communities, polluting the shores with fertilizers, toxic metals, and human waste. Unfortunately, she contends, policy makers seem more interested in promoting trade than protecting the marine environment. McGinn is a senior researcher for the Worldwatch Institute.

As you read, consider the following questions:
1. In McGinn's opinion, what warning signs show that the world's oceans are perilously close to their natural limits?
2. To what do experts link recent outbreaks of severe red tides, in the author's view?
3. According to the author, what areas would experience unimaginable human costs if in 2100 sea levels rise as predicted?

Anne Platt McGinn, "Oceans Are on the Critical List," *USA Today*, vol. 128, January 2000, p. 32. Copyright © 2000 by the Society for the Advancement of Education. Reproduced by permission.

Oceans function as a source of food and fuel, a means of trade and commerce, and a base for cities and tourism. Worldwide, people obtain much or their animal protein from fish. Ocean-based deposits meet one-fourth of the world's annual oil and gas needs, and more than half of world trade travels by ship. More important than these economic figures, however, is the fact that humans depend on oceans for life itself. Harboring a greater variety of animal body types (phyla) than terrestrial systems and supplying more than half of the planet's ecological goods and services, the oceans play a commanding role in the Earth's balance of life.

Due to their large physical volume and density, oceans absorb, store, and transport vast quantities of heat, water, and nutrients. The oceans store about 1,000 times more heat than the atmosphere does, for example. Through processes such as evaporation and photosynthesis, marine systems and species help regulate the climate, maintain a livable atmosphere, convert solar energy into food, and break down natural wastes. The value of these "free" services far surpasses that of ocean-based industries. Coral reefs alone, for instance, are estimated to be worth $375,000,000,000 annually by providing fish, medicines, tourism revenues, and coastal protection for more than 100 countries.

Troubled Waters

Despite the importance of healthy oceans to our economy and well-being, we have pushed the world's oceans perilously close to—and in some cases past—their natural limits. The warning signs are clear. The share of overexploited marine fish species jumped from almost none in 1950 to 35% in 1996, with an additional 25% nearing full exploitation. More than half of the world's coastlines and 60% of the coral reefs are threatened by human activities, including intensive coastal development, pollution, and overfishing.

In January, 1998, as the United Nations was launching the Year of the Ocean, more than 1,600 marine scientists, fishery biologists, conservationists, and oceanographers from across the globe issued a joint statement entitled "Troubled Waters." They agreed that the most pressing threats to ocean health are human-induced, including species overexploitation, habitat degradation, pollution, introduction of alien species, and climate change. The impacts of these five threats are exacerbated by poorly planned commercial activities and coastal population growth.

Yet, many people still consider the oceans as not only inexhaustible, but immune to human interference. Because scientists just recently have begun to piece together how ocean systems work, society has yet to appreciate—much less protect—the wealth of oceans in its entirety. Indeed, current courses of action are rapidly undermining this wealth. . . .

A Sea of Problems

The primary threats to oceans are largely human-induced and synergistic. Fishing, for example, has drastically altered the marine food web and underwater habitat areas. Meanwhile, the ocean's front line of defense—the coastal zone—is crumbling from years of degradation and fragmentation, while its waters have been treated as a waste receptacle for generations. The combination of overexploitation, the loss of buffer areas, and a rising tide of pollution has suffocated marine life and the livelihoods based on it in some areas. Upsetting the marine ecosystem in these ways has, in turn, given the upper hand to invasive species and changes in climate.

Overfishing poses a serious biological threat to ocean health. The resulting reductions in the genetic diversity of the spawning populations make it more difficult for the species to adapt to future environmental changes. The orange roughy, for instance, may have been fished down to the point where future recovery is impossible. Moreover, declines in one species can alter predator-prey relations and leave ecosystems vulnerable to invasive species. The overharvesting of triggerfish and pufferfish for souvenirs on coral reefs in the Caribbean has sapped the health of the entire reef chain. As these fish declined, populations of their prey—sea urchins—exploded, damaging the coral by grazing on the protective layers of algae and hurting the local reef-diving industry.

These trends have enormous social consequences as well. The welfare of more than 200,000,000 people around the world who depend on fishing for their income and food security is severely threatened. As the fish disappear, so do the coastal communities that depend on fishing for their way of life. Subsistence and small-scale fishers, who catch nearly half of the world's fish, suffer the greatest losses as they cannot afford to compete with large-scale vessels or changing technology. Furthermore, the health of more than 1,000,000,000 poor consumers who depend on minimal quantities of fish to constitute their diets is at risk as an ever-growing share of fish—83% by value—continues to be exported to industrial countries each year.

Choosing Poor Strategies

Despite a steadily growing human appetite for fish, large quantities are wasted each year because the fish are under-sized or a nonmarketable sex or species, or because a fisher does not have a permit to catch them and must therefore throw them out. The United Nations' Food and Agricultural Organization estimates that discards of fish alone—not counting marine mammals, seabirds, and turtles—total 20,000,000 tons. equivalent to one-fourth of the annual marine catch. Many of these fish do not survive the process of getting entangled in gear, being brought on board, and then tossed back to sea.

Another threat to habitat areas stems from trawling, with nets and chains dragged across vast areas of mud, rocks, gravel, and sand, essentially sweeping everything in the vicinity. By recent estimates, all the ocean's continental shelves are trawled by fishers at least once every two years, with some areas hit several times a season. Considered a major cause of habitat degradation, trawling disturbs bottom-dwelling communities as well as localized species diversity and food supplies.

The Human Assault

The conditions that make coastal areas so productive for fish—proximity to nutrient flows and tidal mixing and their place at the crossroads between land and water—also make them vulnerable to human assault. Today, nearly 40% of the world lives within 60 miles of a coastline. As more people move to coastal areas and further stress the seams between land and sea, coastal ecosystems are losing ground.

Human activities on land cause a large portion of offshore contamination. An estimated 44% of marine pollution comes from land-based pathways, flowing down rivers into tidal estuaries, where it bleeds out to sea; an additional 33% is airborne pollution that is carried by winds and deposited far off shore. From nutrient-rich sediments, fertilizers, and human waste to toxic heavy metals and synthetic chemicals, the outfall from human society ends up circulating in the fluid and turbulent seas.

Excessive nutrient loading has left some coastal systems looking visibly sick. Seen from an airplane, the surface waters of Manila Bay in the Philippines resemble green soup due to dense carpets of algae. Nitrogen and phosphorus are necessary for life and, in limited quantities, can help boost plant productivity, but too much of a good thing can be bad. Excessive nutrients build up and create conditions that are conducive to outbreaks of dense algae blooms, also known as "red tides." The blooms block sunlight, absorb dissolved oxygen, and disrupt food-web dynamics. Large portions of the Gulf of Mexico are now considered a biological "dead zone" due to algal blooms.

The frequency and severity of red tides has increased in the past couple of decades. Some experts link the recent outbreaks to increasing loads of nitrogen and phosphorus from nutrient-rich wastewater and agricultural runoff in poorly flushed waters.

Adding Dangerous Chemicals

Organochlorines, a fairly recent addition to the marine environment, are proving to have pernicious effects. Synthetic organic compounds such as chlordane, DDT, and PCBs are used for everything from electrical wiring to pesticides. Indeed, one reason they are so difficult to control is that they are ubiquitous. The organic form of tin (tributyltin), for example, is used in most of the world's marine paints to keep barnacles, seaweed, and other organisms from clinging to ships. Once the paint is dissolved in the water, it accumulates in mollusks, scallops, and rock crabs, which are consumed by fish and marine mammals.

As part of a larger group of chemicals known collectively as persistent organic pollutants (POPs), these compounds are difficult to control because they do not degrade easily. Highly volatile in warm temperatures, POPs tend to circulate toward colder environments where the conditions are more stable, such as the Arctic Circle. Moreover, they do not dissolve in water, but are lipid-soluble, meaning that they accumulate in the fat tissues of fish that are then consumed by predators at a more concentrated level.

POPs have been implicated in a wide range of animal and human health problems—from suppression of immune systems, leading to higher risk of illness and infection, to disruption of the endocrine system, which is linked to birth defects and infertility. Their continued use in many parts of the world poses a threat to marine life and fish consumers everywhere.

The Impact of Global Warming

Because marine species are extremely sensitive to fluctuations in temperature, changes in climate and atmospheric conditions pose high risks to them. Recent evidence shows that the thinning ozone layer above Antarctica has allowed more ultraviolet-B radiation to penetrate the waters. This has affected photosynthesis and the growth of phytoplankton and macroalgae. The effects are not limited to the base of the food chain. By striking aquatic species during their most vulnerable stages of life and reducing their food supply at the same time, increases in UV-B could have devastating impacts on world fisheries production.

Because higher temperatures cause water to expand, a warming world may trigger more frequent and damaging storms. Ironically, the coastal barriers, seawalls, jetties, and levees that are designed to protect human settlements from storm surges likely exacerbate the problem of coastal erosion and instability, as they create deeper inshore troughs that boost wave intensity and sustain winds.

Depending on the rate and extent of warming, global sea levels may rise as much as three feet by 2100—up to five times as much as during the last century. Such a rise would flood most of New York City, including the entire subway system and all three major airports. Economic damages and losses could cost the global economy as much as $970,000,000,000 in 2100, according to the Organisation for Economic Co-operation and Development. The human costs would be unimaginable, especially in the low-lying, densely populated river deltas of Bangladesh, China, Egypt, and Nigeria.

The Oceans Are Not Perceived to Be in Immediate Danger

The oceans are not perceived to be in immediate danger, and the need for action to protect the oceans is not readily apparent.

• When asked about the health of the open, deep oceans and of coastal waters and beaches, close to half of the public (46%) reports that they do not know enough about the open oceans to give an opinion and slightly over a quarter (27%) say so for coastal waters.

• Nearly four in ten Americans (39%) rate the health of coastal waters and ocean beaches as "only fair," a quarter (25%) say they are good or excellent, and only one in ten (11%) say poor.

• Damage to the oceans is considered second-tier environmental problem when compared to other environmental problems. Two in ten (19%) Americans report that damage being done to the open, deep oceans is an extremely serious problem. A quarter (24%) report that damage to coastal waters is extremely serious and two in ten (22%) report the same for damage to ocean beaches. These threats to the oceans are seen as less serious than air (31%) and water (36%) pollution and toxic waste (36%), and about as serious as global climate change (21%), species extinction (23%), and overconsumption of resources in the U.S. (24%).

Ocean Project, results of national survey, November 1999.

These damages could be just the tip of the iceberg. Warmer temperatures would likely accelerate polar ice cap melting and could boost this rising wave by several feet. Just four years after a large portion of Antarctica melted, another large ice sheet fell off into the Southern Sea in February, 1998, rekindling fears than global warming could ignite a massive thaw that would flood coastal areas worldwide. Because oceans play such a vital role in regulating the Earth's climate and maintaining a healthy planet, minor changes in ocean circulation or in its temperature or chemical balance could have repercussions many orders of magnitude larger than the sum of human-induced wounds.

While understanding past climatic fluctuations and predicting future developments are an ongoing challenge for scientists, there is clear and growing evidence of the overuse—indeed abuse—that many marine ecosystems and species are suffering from direct human actions. The situation is probably much worse, for many sources of danger are still unknown or poorly monitored. The need to take preventive and decisive action on behalf of oceans is more important than ever.

Saving the Oceans

Scientists' calls for precaution and protective measures are largely ignored by policymakers, who focus on enhancing commerce, trade, and market supply and look to extract as much from the sea as possible, with little regard for the effects on marine species or habitats. Overcoming the interest groups that favor the status quo will require engaging all potential stakeholders and reformulating the governance equation to incorporate the stewardship obligations that come with the privilege of use.

Fortunately for the planet, a new sea ethic is emerging. From tighter dumping regulations to recent international agreements, policymakers have made initial progress toward the goal of cleaning up humans' act. Still, much more is needed in the way of public education to build political support for marine conservation.

To boost ongoing efforts, two key principles are important. First, any dividing up of the waters should be based on equity, fairness, and need as determined by dependence on the resource and the best available scientific knowledge, not simply on economic might and political pressure. In a similar vein, resource users should be responsible for their actions, with decisionmaking and accountability shared by stakeholders and government officials. Second, given the uncertainty in scientific knowledge and management capabilities, it is necessary to err on the side of caution and take a precautionary approach. . . .

The fact that oceans are so central to the global economy

and to human and planetary health may be the strongest motivation for protective action. Although the range of assaults and threats to ocean health are broad, the benefits that oceans provide are invaluable and shared by all. These huge bodies of water represent an enormous opportunity to forge a new system of cooperative, international governance based on shared resources and common interests. Achieving these far-reaching goals, however, begins with the technically simple, but politically daunting, task of overcoming several thousand years' worth of ingrained behavior. It requires seeing oceans not as an economic frontier for exploitation, but as a scientific frontier for exploration and a biological frontier for careful use.

For generations, oceans have drawn people to their shores for a glimpse of the horizon, a sense of scale, and awe at nature's might. Today, oceans offer careful observers a different kind of awe—a warning that humans' impacts on the Earth are exceeding natural bounds and in danger of disrupting life. Protection efforts already lag far behind what is needed. How humans choose to react will determine the future of the planet. Oceans are not simply one more system under pressure—they are critical to man's survival. As Carl Safina writes in *The Song for the Blue Ocean*, "we need the oceans more than they need us."

| *"There is some good news in the marine environment."*

Human Efforts Are Improving the Condition of the World's Oceans and Coastal Regions

Frank E. Loy

In the following viewpoint Frank E. Loy argues that conservation efforts provide hope for the world's oceans and coastal areas. According to Loy, people now realize that ocean resources are not unlimited. As a result, rather than exploiting scarce resources, people are looking for better ways to conserve them. The United States and other nations have negotiated mutual agreements to protect endangered species and ban destructive fishing techniques, he claims. Loy is undersecretary for Global Affairs, U.S. Department of State.

As you read, consider the following questions:

1. According to Loy, how much was dolphin mortality reduced in the eastern Pacific tuna fishery as a result of an agreement between the United States and seven other countries?
2. In the author's opinion, why do efforts to protect the oceans necessarily involve international collaboration?
3. How will the International Commission for the Conservation of Atlantic Tunas (ICCAT) punish rogue nations and vessels that do not observe ICCAT's conservation measures, in the author's view?

Frank E. Loy, lecture at the University of Virginia Center for Oceans Law and Policy, May 11, 1999.

It's been about 30 years since the American environmental movement got started in earnest.

And since that first Earth Day in 1970, we've taken action against all manner of environmental problems—air pollution, water pollution, wildlife loss, hazardous waste and many others. Until fairly recently, though, it seemed that no one was paying the kind of attention to the oceans that they deserved. It seemed unthinkable that the depredations of humanity could have an appreciable effect on something so vast. The oceans seemed infinite.

In 1956, a marine biologist wrote: "It may be rash to put any limit on the mischief of which man is capable, but it would seem that those hundred and more million cubic miles of water . . . is the great matrix that man can hardly sully and cannot appreciably despoil."

As the 20th Century draws to a close, there is a growing awareness that such thinking is naive, and that the oceans are not impervious to our assaults. There has, in fact, been a marked and salutary change in the way interested people think about the oceans. Where we once were concerned about how best to exploit them, we now concentrate more on how best to conserve and protect them. [The] designation [of 1998] as the "Year of the Ocean" is probably the best-known manifestation of this.

The Status of the Oceans

Nonetheless, there remain serious problems in the marine environment. Overfishing, marine pollution, destruction of wetlands, coral reefs and other marine ecosystems are still occurring to alarming degrees.

According to the UN Food and Agriculture Organization [FAO], about two-thirds of the world's fisheries have been fished to or beyond their ability to sustain themselves. Interestingly, the total global catch has remained relatively stable in terms of volume; but we're catching different species now—fishing down the food chain, you might say. As stocks of commercially valuable fish such as cod, pollock and bluefin tuna become depleted, fishers start looking for species that they used to call trash fish—dogfish, skate, monkfish and others.

On the high seas, there are simply too many boats chasing too few fish. And many of them have had the benefit of government subsidies that help them fish even more unsustainably, such as by using sophisticated equipment that maximizes their catch.

Swordfish and tuna fishers, for example, use long-lines—high-strength fishing lines that string out 20 miles or more behind the boat and carry as many as 3,000 baited hooks. Long-lines don't just maximize the catch of the targeted species, they maximize the "by-catch" of myriad other species. According to the National Marine Fisheries Service, about half the marine life that's caught with long-lines is "by-catch"—stuff the fisher doesn't want—and is thrown back into the water. And most of what's thrown back is dead.

And that's all legal. There is, in addition, a growing scourge of illegal fishing and illegal trade in seafood and other marine products. Asian crime syndicates—primarily Chinese—are heavily involved in poaching abalone, for example. South African officials last year confiscated 13,000 abalone that had been illegally taken.

The Problem of Pollution

As the world's population continues to migrate toward the coasts—about a third of the world's people now live within 60 miles of a coastline—the toll of land-based pollution gets worse. Almost half of marine pollution flows into the sea from rivers and estuaries. Another third of marine pollution turns out to be airborne—carried by the wind and deposited far out to sea.

Unfortunately, cleaning up the immediately adjacent land areas—an absolutely necessary step—is not a sufficient cleanup action.

A relatively new addition to the marine environment is the scourge of persistent organic pollutants [POPs], such as DDT and PCBs. POPs migrate by air and fall into the water in the colder regions. POPs are also highly persistent; they don't degrade easily. A recent survey of Baffin Island-based Inuit people, who eat a lot of fish, walrus and seal meat, found dramatically elevated blood levels of two agricultural insecticides that are not used in that region and were banned in the United States in the 1980s.

Another sign of things gone awry is the condition of coral reefs around the world.

In March [1999], the State Department released a really quite alarming report on coral reef bleaching. Put together by two scientists on our staff, the report illuminates a severe bleaching and mortality event that occurred on many reefs around the world—in fact the most severe event of its kind in the modern record. For example, it killed 80 percent of the coral in the reefs around the Seychelles in the Indian Ocean. The report explains that an increase in ocean temperatures brought on by climate change appears to have been the leading culprit.

Coral reefs are among the world's richest, most productive ecosystems. They are also thought to be among the most susceptible to the effects of climate change in that corals are especially sensitive to increased sea surface temperatures.

Thus, it seems that [the 1998] event was not an isolated anomaly, but rather a likely harbinger of things to come: as global temperatures continue to rise, driving sea surface temperatures upward, these bleaching and mortality events are likely to become more frequent and more severe.

The Good News

Lest you mistake me for the grim reaper, let me report that there is some good news in the marine environment.

As I mentioned, there has been a palpable change in our collective understanding of the oceans. And this change is manifest in a number of . . . events.

For example, [in May 1998] the United States and seven other countries signed an agreement to protect dolphins in the eastern Pacific from being harmed or killed by tuna fishing. This agreement has reduced dolphin mortality in that fishery—the only one where dolphins and tuna commingle—by about 98 percent.

The U.S. and other Western Hemisphere governments have also negotiated an agreement to protect endangered sea turtles in the Western Hemisphere from various life-threatening perils, such as drowning in shrimp nets. This has

been the leading cause of a precipitous decline in their numbers. As you may not know, most of what comes up in a
shrimp net is not shrimp. By-catch, which can include turtles, can outweigh the target catch by as much as five-to-
one, and most of the by-catch goes back into the water dead.
But the use of turtle excluder devices, or TEDs, has done a
great deal to protect sea turtles. . . .

Meanwhile, some Indian Ocean nations have expressed an
interest in negotiating a sea turtle agreement for that part of
the world, and we are working closely with them on that.

A Chance to Protect the Ocean

We have a chance now with the ocean that we shouldn't pass
up. Not to bring back a paradise in which we run aground on
oysters and catch fish with buckets, and green turtles guide
us to shore—those days are gone, thanks to our forefathers.
"We really couldn't see what we were doing under the
ocean," says [Jim] Bohnsack [of the National Marine Fisheries Service]. "We could see it on land when the forests were
clear-cut and the buffalo disappeared. It just wasn't obvious
until we couldn't catch cod." Our forefathers could see what
they were doing to the buffalo, but they did it anyway. We
have a chance to be different—to be less ignorant. A hundred
years from now, what will our descendants say about us? It
depends on the ocean we leave them.

Robert Kunzig, *Discover*, January 2002.

We've also made great progress in ridding the seas of
large-scale drift-nets, which, like long-lines, are highly indis-
criminate and destructive. A large drift-net can run as long as
40 miles and will ensnare literally anything that comes into
contact with it, including birds that get entangled in the tops
of the nets at the surface. Thanks to the efforts of this country and others, the UN imposed a moratorium on large-scale
drift-nets in 1993. The moratorium has been quite successful, although we are still negotiating with Italy about the con-
version of its drift-net fleet and we still need to be vigilant
about the use of drift-nets by rogue vessels around the world.

Our new way of thinking about the oceans has significantly changed the tenor of the debate about fish and other
marine resources. Where the fisheries community once ar-

gued about resource allocation—who gets how much of what—we're now focusing more on resource conservation. This has particularly been the case recently in negotiations with Canada over Pacific salmon. A mutual commitment to conservation is now a central feature of those talks. This has not always been the case.

We're also making real progress in marine science. New studies of large marine ecosystems have led to better management of fisheries resources. And research has made us better equipped to identify and discriminate between natural and anthropogenic causes of coastal ecosystem decline, such as in coral reefs.

Using Historic and Existing International Tools

Because the oceans don't respect international boundaries, our efforts to protect them necessarily involve international collaboration. And that collaboration, in turn, depends on available diplomatic tools.

As most of you know, the most basic of those is the 1982 Law of the Sea Convention and the accompanying 1994 agreement on the Part XI deep sea-bed mining provisions—a comprehensive framework for governing and managing the use of the oceans. It reflects a global consensus on the extent to which countries can exercise jurisdiction over their coastal waters. And it spells out the rights and obligations of countries with regard to marine resource conservation (both in coastal waters and on the high seas) and with regard to avoidance of marine pollution from all sources.

The Law of the Sea Convention is widely accepted, some 130 countries having ratified it. That number includes most of the world's wealthier, developed countries, but unfortunately, not this one. Our ratification requires the Senate's approval, which has yet to materialize. Not being a party to it deprives us of a seat at the table when other governments are making the rules that will govern resource exploration and exploitation—by all companies, including our own—in deep sea-bed areas beyond national jurisdiction. Our absence also deprives us of a leadership role in protecting the navigational freedoms that are so vital to our economic and national security interests.

At the same time, however, we are part of a system of more specific marine environmental agreements, via the International Maritime Organization. The IMO has responsibility for more than 35 agreements that address marine pollution, safety, liability and shipping. And we are negotiating new arrangements and strengthening old ones.

The U.S. is also an active participant in a number of regional programs that operate under the auspices of the UN Environment Program. They generally deal with more localized marine pollution problems, such as in the Caribbean or the South Pacific. Pending before the Senate, for example, is the agreement establishing the South Pacific Regional Environment Program. This would establish an intergovernmental organization to promote cooperation in the South Pacific region and protect and improve the environment. We'd like to see action on this convention in the near future.

Agenda 21, the global environmental action plan that came out of the 1992 Earth Summit in Rio de Janeiro [Brazil], set out a plan for protecting marine and coastal environments, through sustainable development of coastal areas and other means. And it called for a new global effort to combat land-based sources of ocean pollution. As a result, the U.S. hosted a conference of the UN Environment Program in Washington in 1995, and that conference produced a Global Plan of Action on Protection of the Marine Environment from Land-Based Sources of Pollution.

The United States also launched the International Coral Reef Initiative, a partnership of governments NGOs [nongovernmental organizations], scientists and private interests with a common concern for protecting, managing and monitoring coral reefs.

And, the U.S. is an active participant in a series of regional fisheries organizations and arrangements that manage fisheries around the world.

These are all useful tools, but needless to say, they're not enough.

The Modern Diplomatic Challenge

Repairing the damage that has been visited upon the oceans is a much greater challenge than, say, cleaning up the Chesapeake Bay—not just because the oceans are so huge, but because no one has full authority over them. The EPA [Environmental Protection Agency] can issue a regulation requiring Eastern Shore hog farmers to keep their waste out of the watershed and they have to comply. But there is no parallel on the high seas, which cover two-thirds of the world's surface. No one's in charge.

In the 20 years or so since the negotiation of the Law of the Sea Convention, there has been a very fortunate sea-change, if you will, in the focus of the marine discussion. As I said earlier, the old debates over jurisdiction have for the most part been settled. As we have come to realize the extent of our impact on—and degradation of—the oceans, we've also come to realize that our emphasis has to shift from allocation to conservation. In other words, it is today better understood and appreciated that ocean ecosystems and marine resources—just like all other natural resources—are finite and we need to exploit them in a sustainable fashion.

And since no one's in charge of the high seas, the making of treaties and the use of economic leverage are about the only tools we have for ensuring the civilized and responsible use of ocean resources. Let me list some of the ways in which we must use these tools:

Ensuring Responsible Use

First, we need to become a party to the Law of the Sea Convention. This will, among other things, give us the clout we need to exact responsible behavior from others. This convention is among the administration's highest priorities for Senate approval.

Second, we absolutely must reduce the over-capacity that is wiping out so many of the world's fisheries. A part of that effort has to be to persuade the major fishing powers to phase out the government subsidies they provide their fleets.

At our urging, the FAO has recently developed an action plan for reducing over-capacity and dealing with the subsidies issue. But we are only starting on what will be a long and difficult endeavor. Much more needs to be done.

Third, we have to attack the atavistic problem of flag state control and, in particular, the problem of flags of convenience.

There are simply too many vessels out there flying the flags of states that are unwilling or unable to ensure that they operate in accordance with internationally agreed-upon rules. As our appreciation for conservation over allocation grows, we also realize that rogue nations and vessels can undermine carefully structured and fragile conservation regimes. This will require the development of some new rules of law and the use of economic tools. We've made some progress here. The old rule of sole state flag control on the high seas is starting to give way to broader enforcement and control by others. For instance, responsible nations that are members of some of the regional fisheries conservation agreements will now, on a collective basis, deny market access to fish caught by vessels that don't fish by the rules.

An example: the International Commission for the Conservation of Atlantic Tunas, or ICCAT, found that fishing vessels from non-member states were damaging its efforts to conserve bluefin tuna and swordfish. So, ICCAT developed a response: it identifies non-member countries whose vessels are fishing at cross purposes to ICCAT's conservation measures and it gives those countries a year to clean up their act. If they don't, ICCAT members can, at their discretion, ban imports of bluefin tuna and swordfish from those countries. Since this regime took effect in 1994, ICCAT has identified Belize, Honduras and Panama as irresponsible users of the Atlantic tuna fishery and has authorized import bans against them. And, more recently, ICCAT has found that those same three countries' vessels fish for swordfish in a way that harms that fishery, so they may soon face swordfish trade sanctions as well.

Fourth, we must work to see the Straddling Fish Stocks Agreement put into effect. The U.S. has ratified this agreement, but it's still 10 short of the 30 ratifications it needs to take effect. It offers critical new legal tools to ensure—and enforce—sound management for species that migrate between coastal waters and the high seas, such as tuna.

There are some other initiatives that we can and should take. For example, we should encourage the major fishing nations to ratify, as we have, the 1993 FAO compliance agreement that will establish a new and badly needed database for monitoring all high seas fishing activity. This agreement is 11 short of the 25 ratifications it needs to take effect.

And we must actively encourage and coordinate scientific efforts to monitor and gather information from the marine environment.

*"In 1995, the United Nations called
fisheries 'globally non-sustainable.'"*

The World's Ocean Fisheries Are Seriously Threatened

Carl Safina

In many regions of the world, people depend on fishing to survive, yet overfishing has made many fisheries nonsustainable, claims Carl Safina in the following viewpoint. Rather than discontinue wasteful fishing practices, fishers have increased their fleets and improved their fishing technology, which has further depleted fish populations, argues Safina. Unfortunately, Safina contends, governments tend to focus on short-term economic solutions to protect fishermen rather than long-term solutions that promote sustainable fishing. Safina, who once served on the Mid-Atlantic Fisheries Management Council, is director of the Living Oceans Program at the National Audubon Society and author of *Song for the Blue Ocean.*

As you read, consider the following questions:

1. According to Safina, in what ways will aquaculture increase habitat loss and degradation?
2. In the author's opinion, why did fishing become an inefficient venture?
3. What examples does Safina provide to support his claim that plucking hard on strings in the food web can cause vibrations in other creatures?

Carl Safina, "Renewing the World's Fisheries," *People & the Planet*, October 10, 2000. Copyright © 2000 by *People & the Planet*. www.peopleandplanet.net. Reproduced by permission.

In the twentieth century, ocean fish catches increased twenty-five fold, from 3 million metric tons to a peak of about 82 million metric tons in 1989. It declined the next year and has generally stagnated since despite increased fishing effort.

All major regions in the Atlantic, Mediterranean, and Pacific, have declining catches. In some regions, catches peaked in the early 1970s and have since declined by more than 50 per cent. In much of the rest of the world, catches peaked in the 1980s and have since declined by 10 to 30 per cent. Only in the Indian Ocean has the catch been increasing as the same industrialised fishing that depleted other oceans develops there.

Few believe the global catch can expand significantly. In 1995, the United Nations called fisheries "globally non-sustainable." They noted, "It is important to continue to single out overfishing (and its economic counterpart, over-investment) as the main culprit."

Meanwhile, some of the world's greatest "inexhaustible" fishing grounds and marine ecosystems—notably the Grand Banks and Georges Bank of Canada and New England—are now largely closed following their collapse. In Newfoundland, shutdowns have entailed a government bailout that will cost nearly two billion dollars. Conservation issues are often pitched as "jobs versus the environment," but in the oceans conservation can make jobs.

People generally forget that fish are wildlife. So instead of sensibly living off the biological interest of wild populations, we have been mining their capital. Ironically, over-emphasis on short-term economics has resulted in losses of billions of dollars to fishing businesses and taxpayers subsidising those losses. We have stretched the oceans to their limits, resulting in depletion, ecological upheaval, human impoverishment, and threat to the food supply for many poor people around the world.

Depending on Fish

Fishing accounts for only about one per cent of the global economy. But on a regional basis, marine fishing contributes enormously to human survival. In Asia, more than one billion people rely on fish as their main source of animal protein. Worldwide, about 200 million people depend on fishing for their livelihoods, and fishing has been termed the "employer of last resort" in the developing world; an occupation when there are no other options.

Shirvanian. © by Vahan Shirvanian. Reprinted with permission.

Each year the number of people increases by an amount equal to the population of Mexico. Even if the fish that now go to fertilisers and animal feeds—a third of the catch—went to people, aquacultural production—seafood farming—will have to double in the next 15 years. Aquaculture has been growing rapidly enough to compensate for the decline of wild fish in commerce. However, since aquaculture requires property ownership and exports most of its expensive production to developed countries, increasing aquaculture may actually mean less food for truly hungry people.

Aquaculture faces challenges of its own. Half the people of the world live within about 60 miles of the coasts. This affects water quality. Worldwide mollusc production has already stagnated because of water quality problems. And many fish that cannot currently be bred are raised in captivity from wild fry which are getting scarce for some species because the wild fish are declining.

Aquaculture does not appear likely to take much pressure off wild populations. In fact, some shrimp farmers are now fishing with fine mesh nets to catch whatever they can to feed their shrimp. Aquaculture is likely to increase habitat losses and degradation. One major reason half the world's mangroves have been cut was to make artificial ponds to grow shrimp—for export to wealthy countries. Intensive aquaculture is in itself a source of pollution, releasing excess feed and faeces in semi-enclosed areas and creating over-nutrification and oxygen deficiencies in waterways. There have been problems with disease in dense, monoculture fish facilities adjacent to wild fish populations. Also problematic are the overuse of antibiotics which are toxic to some wild organisms. And alien species, including pathogens, have been introduced both intentionally and unintentionally during aquaculture activities, severely affecting some wild populations.

A War on Fishes

After World War II, fisheries adapted military detection technologies such as radar, sonar and loran to peaceful efforts of food gathering. But from the fishes' perspective it might have seemed that war was suddenly declared on them. Later came satellite maps of water temperature fronts, indicating where fish are congregating. Some satellites can now detect fish directly.

The arms of the fishing industry grew so full of new gadgets that they could not simultaneously embrace the concept of limits. Between 1970 and 1990, the world's fleet doubled. It now has twice the fishing power needed to catch what the oceans can produce. Consequently, fishing became an extremely inefficient venture, so bloated with excess killing capacity that $124 billion is spent to catch $70 billion worth of fish. Subsidies such as fuel tax exemptions, price controls, low interest loans, and outright grants for gear or infrastructure, plug most of the $54 billion deficit. The United Nations notes that current world fleet cost cannot be matched by revenues at any level of effort. This marginalisation of profitability increases political pressure to keep catches too high.

Subsidies often arise from governments' efforts to preserve employment, something that could be more easily achieved by directing investment away from industrialised, highly mechanised ships and toward smaller boats. Per million dollars of investment, small-scale fisheries employ between 60 and 3,000 persons, while industrial-scale fishing operations employ one to five persons.

The Problem of Bycatch and Habitat

Fishes whose populations are at their historic lows include some very familiar table fare: swordfish, several species of tunas, red snapper, northern cod, several types of flounders, many groupers, and others. But overfishing is not the only problem.

Each year the fishing boats of the world draw up an estimated 27 million metric tons of marine life—about one-quarter to one-third of total catch—which, dying or dead, are thrown overboard. Bycatch includes non-target fishes, juvenile target fishes, seabirds, marine mammals, and any other unintended creatures. Bycatch exceeds target catch in some fisheries. Shrimp trawlers' bycatch outweighs the shrimp themselves by 100 to over 800 percent.

Waste is not the only issue; using everything would not solve the biological effects of catching large numbers of young fish, seabirds, sea turtles and mammals. Plucking hard on certain strings in the food web can cause vibrations in other creatures. In the Shetland Islands during the 1980s, terns, puffins, and other birds failed to breed when a fishery was developed to catch a small prey fish called the sand lance, upon which the birds relied heavily for food. In Kenya, fish that preyed on coral-eating urchins were depleted, allowing urchins to explode and damage the reefs.

In addition, fisheries suffer from habitat destruction and pollution. In many regions, bottom dwelling animals and plants (many of which feed and shelter fish) have been seriously damaged by commercial trawl fishing itself. Throughout the Indo-Pacific, many divers now catch reef fish for export to China by stunning them with cyanide, a potent poison which kills corals that are the fishes' habitats.

Habitats have also been degraded by activities unrelated to fishing. Roughly two-thirds of commercially valuable fish spend their early life in shallow coastal waters, but half the world's estuarine saltmarshes have been destroyed. Destruction of half the world's coastal mangrove forests costs five million tons of annual fish catch—more than six per cent of the world total. Agriculture, road building, and deforestation cause extensive land erosion and sedimentation of coral reefs and streams, while water diversions and dams have destroyed many salmon and sturgeon populations.

A Matter of Poor Management

Few countries have achieved any success in fisheries management. In many regions, there are no data for management. Where data exist, policy-makers often ignore it. In many areas fisheries proceed unmonitored. Where management exists, managers often fail to anticipate new markets and new fishing methods, or, fishers break the rules.

The United Nations says that 70 per cent of the populations of fish, crustaceans, and molluscs in the world's oceans "are in need of urgent corrective conservation and management." Their main concern, at the global level, "is to control fishing effort and to reduce it where necessary." But between 1989 and 1992, the world added 136,000 fishing vessels. Correcting the situation will mean reductions in fishing, requiring controversial decisions, political will and enforcement—exactly the things most governments find difficult.

Solutions are available. One of the most important would be to remove subsidies that prop up fisheries the resources cannot support. There are promising new advances in by-catch reduction devices, and recoveries of some depleted species show that fish can come back. The problems are largely a matter of political will, but politics reflects public opinion, and that means politics can be changed.

The oceans remain the great frontiers of Earth, offering scientific mysteries and compelling opportunities in super-abundance. But the end of a long era of mythical limitless-ness and ideological freedom in the sea is upon us. This may seem a tragedy of sorts, but coming to grips with reality is always liberating in the end.

"Many fisheries are healthy, and recent evidence indicates that even those that have been stressed may be remarkably resilient."

Private Conservation Offers Hope for Ocean Fisheries

Michael De Alessi

In the following viewpoint Michael De Alessi argues that fisheries are resilient, and if private conservation strategies are encouraged, they can recover. When the government intervenes to rescue depleted fisheries, De Alessi claims, the fishers are not held responsible for their actions, so they are not motivated to conserve it. When fishers own the fishery, however, they conserve it because they bear the cost of its depletion. The success of private conservation efforts argues for private stewardship rather than government intervention, he asserts. De Alessi is director of the Center for Private Conservation.

As you read, consider the following questions:
1. In De Alessi's opinion, how do institutions influence the outlook for marine fisheries?
2. How has government intervention in response to fish depletion affected the relationship between the steward and the exploiter, in De Alessi's view?
3. According to the author, how do private property rights create conservation incentives?

Although there has been a significant and disturbing decline in many important fish stocks over the years, the news is hardly all bad. Many marine resources are healthy and well protected, and a growing number of conservation initiatives are shedding light on just how and why some resources are successfully protected and others are pillaged.

Although some species of fish have suffered serious declines in certain areas, extrapolating in a straight-line fashion from these examples is a mistake. The World Wildlife Fund's recent declarations, "Nearly everywhere fisheries have suffered catastrophic declines," and claimed "Without a doubt we have exceeded the limits of the seas," are too broad. Greenpeace also goes too far when it says that due to overfishing, "nature's balance is being altered across vast areas of the world's oceanic ecosystems in ways that may be irreversible."

If one considers only the plight of the Atlantic cod, it is tempting to agree with these sentiments. Cod are one of the world's most fecund fishes (an average female produces 1 million eggs) and have been a staple of many diets for centuries. Cod has even been called the "beef of the sea." Today, however, the cod fishery in New England and Atlantic Canada is the prototypical example of catastrophic fishery decline. Once one of the world's richest fishing grounds, cod are so scarce there now that they are close to commercial extinction.

Two Divergent Views

Although cod fishery is certainly not an isolated example, there is also a rosier view. Many fisheries are healthy, and recent evidence indicates that even those that have been stressed may be remarkably resilient. Based on a slowed, but still increasing world fish catch, the late economist Julian Simon even went so far as to claim that "No limit to the harvest of wild varieties of seafood is in sight."

Proponents of the divergent views of such optimists as Julian Simon and such pessimists as Greenpeace are often referred to as the doomsayers and the cornucopians; surely they both go too far. The world harvest of marine species *has* risen slowly in the last few years, but the increase has come primarily from harvests of lower-value species and the discovery of new stocks.

What both sides ignore is fundamentally important: the role of institutions—the laws and social norms that constrain the behavior of individuals and groups. If the incentives created by these institutions favor unhampered extraction of fish from the sea, then the prospect for that targeted marine life will be bleak. If, on the other hand, these institutions provide incentives for conservation and stewardship, then the outlook for these fish stocks will be bright.

Searching for Solutions

There is no single answer as to how to conserve the ocean's resources. However, experience shows that when people are given the opportunity to conserve marine resources, they generally do. On the other hand, when leaving fish in the water simply means letting someone else catch them, far fewer fish get left in the water. Resource conservation is not happenstance; it is a rational response to a given situation.

Institutional constraints determine these responses, and are intrinsically bound to the question of who owns the rights to do what with a resource. Thus, property rights (rights to such things as the use of a resource, the income derived from a resource, and the ability to transfer part or all of these rights) are a crucial element in any analysis of why some resources are conserved and others are not. The structure of property rights affects behavior because it establishes different allocations of benefits and harms among individuals. Any attempt to exert control over a resource is an attempt to define property rights in that resource, whether through regulation, a group rule, or a form of exclusive ownership.

In the absence of any institutional constraints (a situation commonly referred to as *open access*), each user will tend to extract as much as possible, regardless of the consequences for the resource, because they bear only a fraction of the harms (for example, a degraded fishery for everyone) but reap all of the benefits (that is, the fish they haul up on deck). Thus, a crucial element of conservation is that anyone depleting a resource bears the full consequences of that harm (or, conversely, captures the benefits of conserving the resource). In other words, both positive and negative effects must be internalized.

Responses to Depletion

Open access does not cause problems when fish are plentiful and catches are small, but as the pressure on a fishery grows, so does the potential for depletion. Thus, as pressures on resources increase, open-access regimes become rarer, and property rights wind up either held publicly by government or privately by groups or individuals.

The most common response to open access and depletion has been government intervention, which normally results in restrictions on fishing gear, effort, and seasons. This relationship separates the steward (the state) from the exploiter (the fisher), who still benefits most from maximizing harvests instead of maximizing the value of the resource.

As the state takes responsibility for the fisheries, it also becomes responsible for taking care of those who depend on the resource. This creates a *moral hazard*, which means that generous government benefits to alleviate hardship today end up encouraging the very behavior that helped to create the misery in the first place. In this case, because of government intervention, fishers bear only a fraction of the consequences of their actions, and their impetus for continuing to deplete the fisheries remains. In fact, it is often stronger. Government regulation all too often encourages the profligate waste of resources, time, effort, and capital. . . .

The Depletion of Public Oyster Beds

The oyster fishery in Maryland was once a great source of industry and a staple of many diets. Oysters in the Chesapeake declined precipitously, despite warnings stretching back well into the [1800s]. As stocks continued to decline over time, the Maryland government continued to increase its involvement in the fishery, presenting a dramatic case of regulatory failure. In fact, it has been said that Maryland has passed more legislation dealing with oysters than with any other issue.

In 1891, William Brooks, a scientist and Maryland Oyster Commissioner in the 1880s, writing about the public nature of the oyster fishery, declared even then that "all who are familiar with the subject have long been aware that our present system can have only one result—extermination."

Brooks recommended creating privately owned oyster beds to encourage oyster cultivation and stewardship, but regulation was chosen instead, resulting in all sorts of restrictions on harvesting, including when, where, by whom, and how. People who made their living from the Chesapeake waters fought over both these restrictions and the oysters themselves so ferociously that gunfights were not uncommon. These skirmishes that took place around the turn of the century are commonly referred to as the *Oyster Wars.*

Today, oyster harvests in Maryland are only 1 percent of what they once were (the diseases Dermo and MSX have exacerbated the problem since the 1970s, but the fundamental damage was done long beforehand).

Restrictions on technology were (and still are) so severe that the Maryland skipjacks that ply certain oyster beds are the last commercial fishing fleet in the United States still powered by sail. As if that weren't arcane enough, the boats are given an exemption on Mondays and Tuesdays when they are allowed to dredge for oysters with a *push*—a small

Oyster Harvests in Maryland, 1870–1993

Source: Maryland Department of Natural Resources, Fisheries Division.

motorized dinghy tied to the back of these large, wooden sailboats. This is all on top of restrictions on the oyster season, minimum size limits for harvestable oysters, specifics for the types of dredges that may be used by different people in different places, and specific demarcations over certain areas that are open to harvesting. Nevertheless, and not surprisingly, the oyster beds remain severely depleted.

The Possibilities of Private Ownership

Private ownership is the alternative to public management that *does* force people to bear the costs of their use of a resource. The crucial determinant for whether a resource is privately owned is whether the welfare of the decision makers is tied to the economic consequences of their decisions. Private property rights must also be well defined, enforceable, and transferable. As private property rights become more well defined, resource stewardship becomes more attractive and, equally, owners bear more of the costs of any rapacious behavior.

Unfortunately, clearly defined and readily enforceable private property rights to marine resources are rare. However, those few examples that do exist strongly support the arguments of theorists who have promoted private property rights in the oceans as a means to improve resource management.

Private ownership institutions cover a wide spectrum ranging from communal to individual ownership. Both private communal and private individual property rights regimes create positive conservation incentives by allowing fishers to receive directly the benefits of conservation, and both allow owners to exclude others, decide how to manage resources, and bear the consequences of these actions. Private communal rights may not be so easily transferable, but in either case, the welfare of either the individual or group is tied directly to the health of the resource. There is no government agency standing ready to ameliorate resource deterioration, thus the fishers who own the resource intimately feel any effect, positive or negative. . . .

In marked contrast to public oyster beds in Maryland or unrecognized communal ownership arrangements, the oyster beds of Washington state are owned in fee simple—completely privately, and with a title to prove it. As a result, harvests of oysters in Washington state look very different from those in Maryland. Additionally, the oysters are harvested by relatively modern means and the beds are often seeded from high-tech hatcheries financed by the oyster growers themselves.

One of the few empirical studies of the effects of the private institutions on marine resources compared oyster beds managed by state regulators with those leased privately in the Chesapeake Bay and the Gulf of Mexico (in the Chesapeake, leased beds are common in Virginia). This study found that the leased oyster beds were healthier, better maintained, and produced larger, better-quality oysters. Leaseholders invested in protecting their oysters and enhancing oyster habitat. One way they did this was by spreading old oyster shells on their beds, providing an ideal substrate for larval oysters to settle on. On public beds, no such steps were taken volun-

Washington State Pacific Oyster Production, 1950–1995

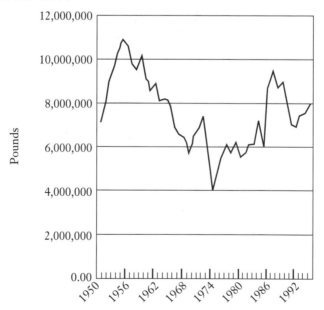

Michael De Alessi, *Earth Report 2000: Revisiting the True State of the Planet.* New York: McGraw-Hill, 2000.

tarily. People who make their living on the water in Maryland were more interested in government-sponsored bailouts and subsidies for oyster bed maintenance than in taking steps on their own to improve harvests. It is possible to lease beds in Maryland, but there has been little interest—once the myriad state-sponsored programs were underway, water folk were loathe to give them up.

A similar dichotomy of approaches and results occurred in England and France, where English oyster beds declined under public regulation, whereas those in France were nurtured by private cultivation.

Individual Transferable Quotas

Although the benefits and feasibility of private ownership are most readily apparent for sedentary species like oysters, they may also be perfectly applicable to more far-ranging species as well. Of course, fisheries are rarely either wholly private or wholly public, but many countries are attempting to improve fisheries management by introducing some limited forms of private ownership into the fisheries, specifically by creating *individual transferable quotas* (ITQs).

Individual transferable quotas grant a right to harvest a certain percentage of the *total allowable catch* (TAC) of fish in a given year, and ITQs can be bought or sold. Over time, ITQs may also offer a real opportunity to move toward the private ownership of marine resources. Over the last few years they have been introduced most notably in New Zealand, Iceland, Australia, the United States, and Canada.

Although they are not really private rights, ITQs can be a tremendous step in the right direction. In contrast to regulation-based controls, they provide positive conservation incentives for those harvesting resources, in large part due to the fact that the health of the fishery is capitalized into the value of the quota. In other words, the brighter the prospects for future harvests, the more ITQs will be worth, allowing ITQ owners to gain now from steps they take to ensure the long-term future health of the fishery. Even some banks are beginning to accept ITQs as collateral, improving access to the fishery by making loans easier to secure for new entrants.

Transforming New Zealand's Fisheries

Until the introduction of ITQs, fisheries management in New Zealand followed a familiar pattern. Since 1960, the government had condoned free entry into the fisheries and subsidized development, producing a predictable result: falling fish stocks and rising investment in fishing boats, nets, and other technologies. The deplorable state of many inshore fisheries led to the Fisheries Act of 1983, which consolidated all previous legislation and, most important, set out to both improve resource conservation and increase economic returns from the fisheries. This led to the creation of tradable quotas for some of the deepwater fisheries and, in 1986, ITQs were introduced for all significant commercial finfish species with the creation of the *quota management system* (QMS).

Today, following numerous improvements, the program appears to be tremendously successful. Fish stocks are generally healthy and ITQs have ended subsidies, reduced fishing capacity, and encouraged investment in scientific research. The New Zealand Ministry of Agriculture's Philip Major described a remarkable transformation after the creation of the ITQ system: "It's the first group of fishers I've ever encountered who turned down the chance to take more fish.". . .

Attention to the world's oceans has been growing in recent years—1997 was the International Year of the Reef and 1998 the International Year of the Ocean. A number of environmental campaigns have also been launched to coincide with these events, aimed at drawing attention to some of the problems that plague the seas.

Unfortunately, although some of these problems are very real, little of this attention has been focused on the institutions that govern fisheries management or the benefits of private conservation and stewardship. From the extreme view of Greenpeace that "the financial captains of the global fishing . . . rush to vacuum the oceans and turn fish into cash," to a more moderate petition [by the Marine Conservation Biology Institute] called "Troubled Water: A Call for Action" that still "paints a dismaying picture" of the destruction of the marine environment, much of the environmental activism in this arena begs for more government involvement instead of less.

Some exceptions are the Marine Stewardship Council, set up by Unilever and the World Wildlife Fund to certify certain fish as caught sustainably, and the Environmental Defense Fund's (EDF) sponsorship of ITQs. The EDF, however, . . . strongly criticized the environmental effects of aquaculture, even though, that, too, is a result of ill-defined ownership and perverse government programs.

Entrepreneurs around the world are not nearly as hesitant to embrace the opportunities afforded by private stewardship. [In 1998], . . . the economist Elmer Keen envisaged vast increases in marine productivity with the extension of private rights into the seas. Today, quota holders in New Zealand are moving in that direction, and an even more ambitious project is underway to fertilize the oceans—only made possible by exclusive access to the fisheries of a small island nation in the Pacific whose fisheries will, of course, benefit.

These are the kinds of visionaries who will continue to offer real solutions to the problems of overfishing and marine habitat degradation. Their impressive results to date suggest that private conservation is the answer to protecting and enhancing the world's marine resources.

"Sea level rise is an equal opportunity destroyer. It will affect low-lying coastal areas throughout the world, regardless of the level of development."

Rising Sea Levels Threaten Coastal Regions

Don Hinrichsen

Some experts believe that sea levels will rise as a result of global warming caused by human activities. Many who inhabit the world's highly populated coastal regions will suffer tremendous economic and social upheaval as a result, asserts Don Hinrichsen in the following viewpoint. In response, according to Hinrichsen, the United States will spend billions of dollars to prevent flooding and protect its water supply, but the world's poorer nations cannot afford these protections and millions will be displaced. Moreover, rising seas will damage coastal ecology and threaten coastal livelihoods, he claims. Hinrichsen is author of *Coastal Waters of the World: Trends, Threats, and Strategies.*

As you read, consider the following questions:

1. According to Hinrichsen, what are the areas most vulnerable to sea level rise?
2. In the author's view, why is the land underneath some coastal cities sinking?
3. According to the author, what assumption defers serious action to protect against the impact of climate change?

Don Hinrichsen, "The Oceans Are Coming Ashore," *World Watch*, vol. 13, November/December 2000, pp. 27–35. Copyright © 2000 by World Watch Institute. Reproduced by permission.

Rising sea levels are eroding the beaches and wetlands of the Chesapeake Bay, the huge inlet along the U.S. mid-Atlantic coast that contains the largest body of brackish water in North America. Maryland, the state that contains most of the bay's shoreline, is now on the front lines of climate change. On the state's eastern shore, the 8,100-hectare Blackwater National Wildlife Refuge has lost close to one-third of its land area over the past three decades, and many once rich bottomland farms are now either waterlogged or too saline to sustain crops. Out in the bay, Maryland's Smith Island—actually a little archipelago 13 kilometers long and 6 kilometers wide—has lost about 490 hectares over the past century; land that was wooded a generation ago is now salt marsh.

More and more of Maryland's natural Shoreline is disappearing behind a bulwark of revetments and bulkheads. According to the the U.S. Environmental Protection Agency (EPA), the permits issued over the past 15 years for this type of construction now account for 500 kilometers of the state's coast. In 1996, a conference at Washington College in Chestertown, Maryland brought together 140 scientists, property owners, and government officials who produced a blunt consensus statement: "The evidence that sea level has risen, is rising and will continue to rise along the coast of Maryland is so great that no informed person would suggest otherwise."

One Billion at Risk

There is no comprehensive global assessment of the number of people who would be displaced by a 1-meter sea level rise, but it's thought that roughly 1 billion people live at sea level or just a few meters above it. Regional studies conducted by the Intergovernmental Panel on Climate Change (IPCC) suggest that the impacts will be devastating, especially in the tropics and warm temperate regions, where many coastlines are heavily settled. The most vulnerable areas are concentrated along the southern coast of the Mediterranean, the west coast of Africa, South Asia (India, Sri Lanka, Bangladesh, and the Maldives), all coastal states comprising Southeast Asia, and low-lying coral atolls in the Pacific and Indian Oceans. These regions contain some of the poorest and most heavily populated countries in the world, with some of the highest fertility levels. Just over 2 billion people inhabit these places and up to half of them live on the equivalent of $2 a day or less. China and Southeast Asia include the most crowded coastlines in the world, with population densities averaging over 2,000 people per square kilometer. All of these regions are primed for profound social upheaval. . . .

When the Seas Invade Cities

Sea level rise is going to be an urban planner's nightmare. In many coastal cities, the problem is compounded by the fact that the land underneath them is sinking. Excessive groundwater pumping is the primary cause of this subsidence, but urban sprawl is a factor too, since buildings and pavement cause rainfall to run off instead of seeping back into the earth to recharge the groundwater. In addition to lowering the ground level, this overpumping makes the cities vulnerable to a kind of underground flooding: as the freshwater is pumped out of coastal aquifers, saltwater tends to seep in. Underground saltwater intrusion is a serious problem for Manila, Dhaka, Bangkok, and Jakarta. Obviously, continued sea level rise will tend to make the aquifers under these cities even saltier. Most of Manila's wells, for instance, might very well turn too saline to use at all if the sea level rises by a meter or so. That would force officials to spend billions of dollars that the Philippines doesn't have on desalination plants. The money would have to be borrowed from abroad, saddling the country with more foreign debt.

Since most of these cities are just a few meters above sea level, they would face another major expense in the need to beef up flood control systems. Manila's system is so antiquated that every year during the monsoon rains, scores of people drown in low-lying areas because the storm drains cannot handle the tremendous volume of water dumped on the city over the course of a few hours. "We are overwhelmed right now," shuddered one city water manager. "I can't even imagine what would happen if the sea rises by a meter. Hundreds would drown during the rainy season and we would be faced with massive capital investments in new, bigger pumping stations and storm drain systems."

Displacing Millions of People

Bangkok's problems are no less severe. Dozens of people living in swampy areas drown every year during the rainy season. Many more are made periodically homeless—most of them squatters occupying squalid, make-shift settlements along the Chao Phraya River and its tributaries, or along the city's many fetid, refuse-choked canals. Officials estimate that sea level rise will cost Bangkok an additional $20 million per year in pumping costs alone. The cost of relocating displaced communities has not been estimated, but is expected to be "astronomical."

In terms of the sheer number of people likely to be affected, Shanghai, China's largest city, may be in a class of misery all its own. A 1-meter rise would flood up to a third of this city of 17 million people, displacing as many as 6 million of them. Shanghai is currently attracting hordes of migrants from all over the Yangtze River Valley; that demographic current would be reversed, as immense waves of refugees flood out of the city.

The Americas

Sea level rise is an equal opportunity destroyer. It will affect low-lying coastal areas throughout the world, regardless of the level of development. Even though the Americas are for the most part better prepared to cope, . . . these nations also face profound dislocation.

In the United States, a study carried out by the U.S. Federal Emergency Management Agency (FEMA) found that a half-meter sea level rise would inundate up to 1.9 million hectares of dry land along the eastern seaboard and Gulf Coast if no protection measures are taken. Up to 1.6 million hectares would be flooded if currently developed areas are protected. These figures do not cover the wetlands that would be affected, but a study by the U.S. Environmental Protection Agency (EPA) estimated that a 1-meter rise would inundate close to 3.6 million hectares, with the losses about equally divided between the wet and dry areas.

The FEMA study also found that a 90-centimeter rise would greatly increase the amount of the east coast floodplain that is vulnerable to storm damage—from 5.1 million to 7

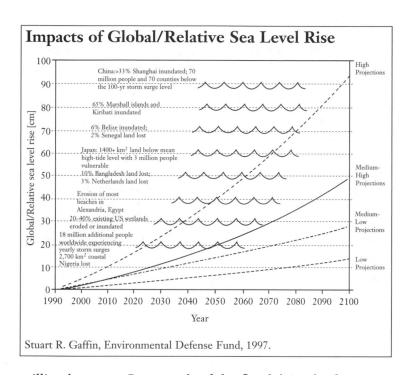

Impacts of Global/Relative Sea Level Rise

China:>33% Shanghai inundated; 70 million people and 70 counties below the 100-yr storm surge level

65% Marshall islands and Kiribati inundated

6% Belize inundated; 2% Senegal land lost

Japan: 1400+ km² land below mean high-tide level with 3 million people vulnerable

10% Bangladesh land lost; 3% Netherlands land lost

Erosion of most beaches in Alexandria, Egypt

20–40% existing US wetlands eroded or inundated

18 million additional people worldwide experiencing yearly storm surges

2,700 km² coastal Nigeria lost

Global/Relative sea level rise [cm]

Year

High Projections

Medium-High Projections

Medium-Low Projections

Low Projections

Stuart R. Gaffin, Environmental Defense Fund, 1997.

million hectares. Over much of the floodplain, the frequency of storm damage would increase radically. A 1-meter rise, for example, would cause areas that are currently inundated only by the once-in-a-century "monster storm" to see such flooding every 15 years. The likely effect would be to push insurance costs beyond the reach of many or most people—depending, of course, on the extent of government subsidies. Overall, according to the EPA study, a 1-meter rise could cost the U.S. economy anywhere from $40 billion to $475 billion.

Similarly, an IPCC study of five east coast Latin American countries—Argentina, Belize, Guyana, Uruguay, and Venezuela—found that a 1-meter rise would inundate around 13.5 million hectares and affect upwards of 750,000 people, the majority of them living in poor fishing communities and squatter settlements. By far the worst effects would be felt by tiny Guyana. Out of a total population of 700,000, about 80 percent or 560,000 people would be affected; at least half would probably end up as environmental refugees.

Biologically rich coastal wetlands, such as mangrove swamps, marshes, salt ponds, and intertidal areas are also endangered by sea level rise. According to studies carried out by the Hadley Centre for Climate Prediction and Research in Britain, 40–50 percent of the world's remaining coastal wetlands will be lost by 2080, due to a combination of drainage for agriculture, urban sprawl, and the effects of a 1-meter sea level rise. And this is the conservative estimate: it assumes that major conservation initiatives will offset some of the loss. In the no-remediation scenario, up to three-quarters of remaining coastal wetlands are lost.

The areas most apt to lose their coastal wetlands differ somewhat from those most at risk in human terms. The coastal wetlands most likely to suffer lie along the Atlantic coast of North and Central America, the U.S. Gulf Coast, and around the Mediterranean and Baltic Seas. These areas generally exhibit an appreciable slope once you move inland from the tidal range. There is little potential in such places for coastal wetlands to migrate inland—they would be trapped between the advancing waves and the high ground. In the United States, studies suggest that up to 43 percent of remaining coastal wetlands would be submerged, mostly along the Atlantic and Gulf coasts. Louisiana is already losing some 900 hectares of coastal wetlands each year to a combination of subsidence and sea level rise. Since nearly half of the world's coastal wetland has already been annihilated by development, the losses inflicted by sea level rise are likely to be far more disruptive than they might otherwise be. Many of these ecosystems will probably not be able to perpetuate themselves as residual fragments of what were once much larger wholes. Their characteristic species will begin to die out; the resulting landscape will be far less diverse and probably less stable.

A Tragedy for All Life

These ecological tragedies will overlap with human tragedies as well, although the connection will be easier to see in some places than in others. Consider the Sunderbans, one of the most vulnerable coastal wetlands in Asia. The largest contiguous mangrove forest in the world, the Sunderbans carpets 100,000 hectares along the Bay of Bengal, partly in India and partly in Bangladesh. It is home to myriad wild creatures, including 315 species of birds; among the endangered species to be found here are the Rhesus macaque (a monkey), Irrawaddy dolphin, and Bengal tiger. A 1-meter sea level rise could well mean extinction for the local populations of many Sunderbans creatures. The Sunderbans tigers, for example, currently number around 350 and are an important reservoir of genetic wealth for their species. The rising waters would probably do away with their main prey animals and drive the tigers into heavily settled areas further inland, where it is unlikely that they would survive.

The Sunderbans is human habitat as well. At least half a million people are directly dependent on the forest—woodcutters, thatch harvesters, fishers, and collectors of honey and beeswax. In the event of substantial sea level rise, most of these people would share the tigers' fate: they would be forced farther inland and their forest economy would be badly crippled.

The Danger of Deferred Action

"We are, in essence, conducting a big geophysical experiment with the Earth's climate," says Sydney Levitus, an oceanographer at the U.S. National Oceanic and Atmospheric Administration. "One of the possibilities is that [the Earth] could go into an abrupt climate shift." Thus far, there is little evidence that this possibility has captured the imaginations of many politicians or policymakers. "Unfortunately, as with most coastal management efforts," says Jens Sorensen, a coastal management expert at the University of Massachusetts in Boston, "most government agencies are doing nothing more than rearranging the deck chairs on the Titanic." The usual assumption seems to be that climate change proceeds by increment, so serious action can be deferred until later in the century. Real reform, in other words, is our children's problem.

No doubt, part of the reason for this complacency is that the climate computer models speak in terms of fractions of degrees—they sound incremental even when they are forecasting convulsive change. And indeed, the prospects of an abrupt shift, in one form or another, no longer seem that remote. For example, over the past three decades, the world's oceans have warmed by an average of 0.3 degrees Centigrade. But tropical waters in the northern hemisphere have been warming at the rate of 0.5 degrees Centigrade per decade, five times the global rate. "This may seem like a small number," says Levitus, "but in fact it represents a huge increase in the heat content of the world ocean." And of course, other parts of the earth's climate system may also be on the verge of rapid flux. This appears to be the case, for example, with the world's ice cover.

Nor is the climate system the only factor in play. Consider the increase in our own numbers. Today, about one-sixth of the global population lives within a few meters above sea level. (These, of course, are the 1 billion people most at risk from sea level rise.) According to mid-range U.N. projections, the global population is expected to grow from its current 6.1 billion to 8.9 billion by 2050. The U.N. also projects that a full third of these people may live in coastal regions subject to the effects of sea level rise. That's the equivalent of nearly half the current global population. Where are these people going to go? Our geophysical experiment, to use Levitus's term, could become an unprecedented social experiment as well. Unfortunately, this scenario differs in one crucial aspect from experiments in the ordinary sense of the word: we won't be able to start over if the results go awry.

| "*People have been given the impression that the 18 cm sea level rise claimed for the 20th century is an observed quantity. . . . It is not.*"

Claims That Sea Levels Are Rising Are Unproven

John L. Daly

In the following viewpoint John L. Daly argues that predictions about rising sea levels due to global warming are based on a theoretical model, not on actual evidence. Measuring sea level is difficult and depends on equipment such as tide gauges that are anything but flawlessly accurate. For example, subsidence caused by the weight of buildings can lower gauges, making it appear that sea levels are rising. In fact, no evidence exists to prove that sea levels are rising. Daly is a science adviser for the Greening Earth Society.

As you read, consider the following questions:
1. According to Daly, how have the Dutch changed the coastline and tidal flow patterns?
2. What does the author say happened to sea levels 10,500 years ago when the ice sheets over Europe and North America melted?
3. In Daly's opinion, what are the weaknesses of the ICE-3G model?

John L. Daly, "Testing the Waters: A Report on Sea Levels," www.co2andclimate. org, 2000. Copyright © 2000 by the Greening Earth Society. Reproduced by permission.

A serious problem confronts any researcher who looks into the question of tides and sea levels, especially in a search for that elusive concept known as "mean sea level," (MSL) or "Zero Point of the Sea."

Not only is it difficult to determine true MSL of any one location, it is even more difficult to detect any changes in that level over time. Imagine attempting to measure mean sea level on a Hawaiian surfing beach. Although sea level and tides work over longer timescales, the essence of the problem is much the same. Study of sea level has now taken on more urgency because of the predictions of sea level rise that might result from any global warming as a consequence of an in-creased atmospheric concentration of carbon dioxide (CO_2).

Climate modelers and the Intergovernmental Panel on Climate Change (IPCC) predict that one of the conse-quences of global warming will be rising sea levels due to thermal expansion of the ocean water mass and the melting of non-polar glaciers. They claim the oceans *already* have risen 18 cm (7 inches) during the 20th century, an annual rate of 1.8 mm per year. They further predict that the oceans will rise approximately a further 50 cm (19½ inches) during the 21st century, an accelerated annual rate of 5 mm per year.

Such predictions have taken on hysterical proportions when policy institutions such as the US Environmental Pro-tection Agency (EPA) readily adopt a *"worse than* worst case" scenario. EPA claims that a 1 meter sea level rise will inun-date 7,000 square miles of dry land, 50–80% of U.S. wet-lands, and cost the U.S. between $270- and $475-billion alone. With a final flourish, they claim their estimates "are almost certainly too low.". . .

Calculating Mean Sea Level

Mean Sea Level is defined as "the mean level of the water surface over a specific long series of measurements. No mat-ter how long a period of data is averaged, the ideal true mean sea level is unattainable because changes are taking place over long and short time scales." Where sea level is mea-sured at only one location, it is sometimes referred to as "Relative Sea Level" (RSL) because the measurement speci-fies the height of the sea in relation to local landmarks. If the land is rising or sinking, it would manifest itself as apparent rises and falls in sea level, even if the actual level of the ocean remains unchanged. Before the advent of satellites, it was impossible to establish a truly global MSL.

As a descriptive term, Mean Sea Level often is used to mean either the MSL at a single location (meaning it is really RSL) or over an entire region. Global MSL ultimately is determined by the quantity of water in the oceans, the temperature of that water, the volume of water stored in the Antarctic and Greenland ice sheets, the volume of water stored as ice in non-polar glaciers, and the quantity of water stored in natural and man-made inland catchments, lakes, and reservoirs.

The standard instrument used to determine MSL and tidal extremes is a tide gauge. A tide gauge measures the height of the sea at regular intervals in order to record the passage of high and low tides, and the harmonics unique to the location where the tide gauge is situated. Most gauges are installed in populated areas throughout the Northern Hemisphere, particularly in Europe and North America. There are relatively few tide gauges accompanied by long records in the Southern Hemisphere. . . .

Evaluating Tide Gauge Errors

Tide gauges, like the instruments used to collect surface temperature data, are subject to several local errors that can distort the data. Just as temperature data is affected by urban heat islands, tide gauges located at major cities or ports also are subject to urbanization—mainly the tendency of large cities to subside due to the weight of the structures and changes in the underground water table. The larger the city, the greater is the tendency toward subsidence. This is a creeping effect that, over time, will manifest itself at a tide gauge as a rise in relative sea level. Cities located on alluvial, low-lying coasts are the most affected.

For example, Adelaide in South Australia is showing a strong sea level rise that is not evident at nearby smaller ports (Port Pirie, Port Lincoln, Victor Harbour). The Adelaide anomaly subsequently has been found to be caused by the long-term withdrawal of groundwater beginning with European settlement. It has given rise to localized urban subsidence. A similar example of subsidence is Bangkok, Thailand, where the sea has risen a meter in the last 30 years. But the sea has not really risen; the land is sinking.

A second kind of subsidence error arises from the fact that most tide gauges are mounted on man-made structures, e.g. piers and docks. Over decades, the structures undergo subsidence unless they are built upon bedrock.

In the Netherlands, the tide gauge record from Amsterdam, cited in the IPCC draft report, is the longest in the world. It extends back to 1700. Another Dutch record from Hoek Van Holland dates from 1865. Both show a distinctive long-term sea level rise since the mid–19th century. While this also may be due to urban subsidence, one factor makes all Dutch tide gauge data questionable for use in global sea level studies. The problem has its origin in the saying, "God made the world, but the Dutch made Holland" which acknowledges the extensive reclamation of land from the sea characteristic of centuries of Dutch history.

The Sky Isn't Falling and the Sea Isn't Rising

Global-warming devotees have been making alarmist predictions about the rising sea levels they think will follow an increase in the earth's average temperatures. The horror stories include the flooding of low-lying coastal areas, the disappearance of island nations, the inundation of America by environmental refugees, and an exponential explosion in insurance claims. Activists apparently don't realize that the much-ballyhooed climate models that predict global warming cannot make any quantitative predictions at all about sea levels.

S. Fred Singer, *Wall Street Journal*, November 10, 1997.

Two key variables used to determine tide height are seabed topography and coastal topography. The Dutch extensively have changed both. Over several centuries, the Dutch have reclaimed land from the sea, altering their coastline and permanently altering tidal flow patterns.

During the 20th century, the Dutch reclaimed much of the large inland gulf known as the Zuider Zee and dammed off the rest from the North Sea. Before these coastline changes were made, the area was a large tidal sink. Tidal water flowing up and down the English Channel and North Sea previously could drain in and out of the Zuider Zee. Now it is unable to do so, thus raising local sea level outside the Ijsselmeer Dam, particularly during high tide. The surrounding sea is shallow (typically only 25–30 meters) and makes the entire region tidally sensitive to coastal terraforming of the kind undertaken by the Dutch.

Although the Dutch are among the most strident advocates of the Kyoto Protocol [which hoped to commit industrialized nations to reduce emission of "greenhouse gases"], due to their sensitivity to the prospect of sea level rise, their programs of land reclamation over several centuries may have contributed significantly to the very problem they now perceive as threatening their national interest.

Correcting for Post Glacial Rebound

We have a very different record from Stockholm, Sweden. Clearly, sea level at Stockholm is falling—by about 40 cm (15½ inches) over 110 years—despite the possibility of city subsidence. But here . . . the IPCC portrays Stockholm in the latest Third Assessment Report draft [using] a "detrended" record of the sort that corrects for a phenomenon that places all European and North American tide gauge data in doubt. The phenomenon is known as "Post Glacial Rebound" (PGR). During the last Ice Age, the region in which Stockholm was located was buried under several kilometers of ice. The Ice Age ended about 10,500 years ago with a rapid melting of the ice sheets over Europe and North America. Their melting resulted in sea level rise. And, with the ice gone, the plasticity of the mantle below the solid crust of the earth began to force the crust upward because the dead weight of the ice no longer was present. This process has gone on since the last Ice Age, is happening now, and will continue to do so well into the future.

PGR is underway all over Europe, North America, and east Asia. These are the continents most affected by the enormous ice sheets. Those regions weighed down by ice continue to uplift like Sweden. This, in turn, causes peripheral regions around the margins of the former ice masses to subside as the continental crusts adjust and rebalance to the weight redistribution.

The North Atlantic actually is a huge basin semi-enclosed by continental landmasses. A 1400 nautical mile gap between west Africa and South America connects it to the world's other oceans. This may explain partly why long-term tide gauge records from within that basin are not always consistent with records outside. It also is unfortunate that all the really old tide gauge records (those that extend back into the 19th century) come from Europe—the center of the PGR zone. Later American records are affected similarly. . . .

The ICE-3G Model

As in the case of Stockholm with its sharply falling sea level, IPCC scientists made a massive correction to the data, turning an RSL *fall* into an MSL *rise*. This outcome results from adjusting the observed data with correction factors derived from the ICE-3G model developed by [W.] Peltier and [M.] Tushingham in 1991. Their model purports to describe crustal movements of the continents and seabed in the wake of the demise of the great ice sheets. The model depends on calculations about the plasticity of the earth's mantle upon which the crustal land masses "float."

ICE-3G is the model most used for correcting tide gauge data against PGR. Its creators were among the first scientists to link global sea level rise and the Greenhouse Effect, in 1989 claiming that sea levels were rising at a rate in excess of 1 mm/yr.

An impression has been conveyed to the public, media, and policymakers that the sea level rise of 18 cm in the past century is an *observed* quantity and thus open to little dispute. What is not widely appreciated is that this quantity is largely the product of modeling and *not a product of observation*. It is therefore very much open to dispute, especially when observed sea level data from many parts of the world fail to live up to the IPCC claims.

The ICE-3G model is a global, theoretical treatment used to describe how the ice masses melted and disintegrated at the end of the last Ice Age, and the crust's consequent readjustments under pressure from the lithosphere below. The model has some inherent weaknesses.

• It assumes that when the great ice sheets melted there

was no change in the oceans' surface area. This is wrong of course, because vast areas of the continental margins were flooded as sea level rose. The model's creators acknowledge this, but believe the sea level effect to have been small—something very much in dispute.

- ICE-3G assumes that the mantle and crust were in equilibrium (general balance) before the "big melt" began. This is an unrealistic assumption because the Ice Age was a very dynamic period, geologically.
- The model was calibrated against 192 RSL sites from around the world. However, 169 are in the North Atlantic Basin (including the Arctic). It only lists 18 as from the Pacific Ocean. Most of those were along North America's Pacific Coast. As noted earlier, this is a tectonically active area. Only five sites cover the entire South Atlantic, Indian, and Southern Oceans—nearly two-thirds of the world's oceanic area.
- ICE-3G uses "fudge factors." Where there is a mismatch between the observed RSL site and the model's result, the modeled ice load either is increased in thickness or its melting is delayed. This is reminiscent of a similar procedure used in some of the General Circulation Models used to study climate change where the sun's energy output either is turned up or turned down to stabilize the model at a desired temperature.
- ICE-3G predicts a sea level rise of 115 meters during the de-glaciation. But physical evidence from most other studies places this figure at 120 to 130 meters. Peltier & Tushingham attribute the discrepancy to "missing ice" in regions assumed to have been ice-free but might, in fact, have been glaciated.

A Limited Model

What should be clear is that the ICE-3G global de-glaciation model is really a North Atlantic/Arctic model. Its accuracy must deteriorate therefore as distance increases from the location of the ancient ice sheets, especially for those regions outside the North Atlantic Basin. For the rest of the world's oceans and crust, this model may have little relevance, especially given the paucity of RSL sites from the

Pacific and Southern Hemisphere oceans against which it can be calibrated.

Even within the North Atlantic Basin where ICE-3G could be expected to exhibit its greatest accuracy, a 1996 study of the southeastern seaboard of the U.S. by [J.] Davis and [J.] Mitrovica finds that the model overestimates sea level rise in that region due to incorrect calculation of lower mantle viscosity. From Key West [Florida], to Cape Hatteras [North Carolina], their recalculation of mantle viscosity results in a reduced estimate of sea level rise of between 2.28–1.45 mm per year.

As for the world's four other great oceans, it is not only the model's theoretical elegance that should be judged, but more important, how its application to the sea level problem accords with observed reality. The IPCC estimate of +1.8 mm/yr sea level rise in the 20th century is critically dependent upon the processing of tide gauge data using this model.

Finally, it must be stressed that ICE-3G does not and cannot correct for tectonics such as exist along the Ring of Fire in the Pacific Ocean. It does not and cannot correct for local urban subsidence such as exists in Adelaide [Australia], Venice [Italy], and Bangkok [Thailand]. It does not and cannot correct for subsidence of the man-structures upon which tide gauges are mounted. With or without the ICE-3G model, all of these local errors still exist and make global estimates of sea level change very difficult to validate.

Whatever degree of confidence is placed in this model, to use it in determining past global sea level changes means that the IPCC estimate of +18 cm sea level rise over the last 100 years cannot be regarded as an *observed* value. Rather it is a largely *modeled* value subject to a high margin of error due to local distortions. . . .

An Unsupported Model

People have been given the impression that the 18 cm sea level rise claimed for the 20th century is an observed quantity. It now should be clear that it is not. The 18 cm figure is the product of combining data from tide gauges with the output of the ICE-3G de-glaciation model. A simple logical equation can be constructed for this:

an *observed* quantity ± a *modeled* quantity = a *modeled* quantity

Thus, the claimed 18 cm sea level rise is a model construct, not an observed value. Worse still, the model is primarily focused on the North Atlantic Basin, which exhibits relative sea level trends quite unlike any observed outside the North Atlantic. Thus, global estimates should not be inferred with any confidence from modeled trends that mainly affect only that basin.

In the world's remaining oceans there clearly is a lack of evidence of sea level rise during the 20th century. This is particularly true around the Australian coast—a coastline representative of three oceans—where good quality records of tide gauge data are available. The rise recorded along the Australian coast is an insignificant 1.6 cm for the entire century. That's just over half an inch in a hundred years!

The absence of significant sea level rise around Australia is confirmed by a similar absence of sea level change as measured since 1888 against the Ross-Lempriere benchmark carved on a natural rocky cliff on the Isle of the Dead in Port Arthur, Tasmania. It also is possible that a significant sea level fall occurred between 1841 (when the benchmark was struck) and 1888 (when its height was accurately measured). The only other tide gauge records of similar age are few in number and come from regions severely affected by PGR within the North Atlantic basin. Thus, they cannot be considered as conclusive evidence disputing a possible global sea level fall during that period.

Outside the North Atlantic Basin, most other tide gauges with long-term records have been mounted in tectonically active areas, especially along the west coast of North America and New Zealand. Thus they are unsuitable for measuring global trends. Many others are subject to local subsidence.

As to the future, the IPCC suggests accelerating sea level rise to nearly 5 cm/yr. However, the TOPEX-Poseidon satellites now show sea level rise to be only 0.9 mm/yr, all of which has been attributed to the 1997–98 El Niño event. Sea level was largely unchanged before and after that event. Thus the 0.9 mm/yr rise merely is a statistical artifact and does not represent a true rise in the background sea level.

Finally, it should be remembered that no matter what is

said about sea level, it depends entirely upon how global climate responds to greenhouse gases—whether the planet warms significantly or not. Sea level rise is contingent on atmospheric warming. If there is no warming, there is no sea level rise. The record of atmospheric temperature as recorded by satellites since 1979 reveals no significant warming despite numerous model predictions to the contrary.

Periodical Bibliography

The following articles have been selected to supplement the diverse views presented in this chapter.

Jeffrey Chanton	"Global Warming and Rising Oceans," *Action Bioscience*, October 2002.
John A. Church	"How Fast Are Sea Levels Rising?" *Science*, October 26, 2001.
Dean Travis Clarke	"So Long Oceans. Thanks for All the Fish," *Cruising World*, October 1998.
Robert Constanza	"Principles for Sustainable Governance of the Oceans," *Science*, July 10, 1998.
Greenpeace	"In Hot Water: Global Warming Upsets Natural Balance of Climate and Oceans," *Greenpeace Magazine*, Summer 1998.
Mary Anna Grove	"1998: Year of the Ocean," *ChemEcology*, May 1998.
Thomas Hayden	"Deep Trouble," *U.S. News & World Report*, September 10, 2001.
Don Hinrichsen	"Ocean Planet in Decline," *People & the Planet*, June 7, 2002.
Robert Kunzig	"2001: Year of the Ocean," *Discover*, January 2002.
Bernard Martin	"A Fisherman's Tale," *Our Planet*, November 5, 1998.
D.L. Parsell	"High-Tech Fishing Is Emptying Deep Seas, Scientists Warn," *National Geographic News*, February 26, 2002.
Fred Pearce	"Coral Grief," *Our Planet*, November 3, 1999.
Mark Stuertz	"Fish Story," *Dallas Observer*, July 9, 1998.
Tomari'I Tutangata	"Rising Waters, Falling Hopes," *Toward Freedom*, November 2000.

CHAPTER 2

What Ocean Management and Conservation Practices Should Be Pursued?

Chapter Preface

Conservation efforts in the United States are generally traced to John Muir, who founded the Sierra Club in 1892. Muir wrote a series of books advocating the joys of the wilderness experience, which inspired efforts to conserve wilderness areas so that Americans could enjoy their pristine beauty. However, rising concerns about air and water pollution after World War II began to alter notions of how best to protect the earth. In 1962 Rachel Carson reflected these growing concerns in her book *Silent Spring*, a tale of the pesticide poisoning of man and nature. The book provoked a public outcry. Believing that conservation as advocated by Muir was no longer enough, some conservationists shifted their philosophy to environmentalism, a political movement demanding that the state not only preserve the earth but regulate and punish those who polluted it. As a result of environmental activism, in the 1970s Congress passed several environmental laws. Many environmentalists believe, however, that the government has not done enough, particularly to protect the oceans and marine wildlife. Marine environmental organizations such as Greenpeace have learned to use the public's concern for the environment as a force for change. Consumer boycotts, for example, have become one of several tools these organizations use to conserve the world's oceans.

Boycotts have proven to be effective. In 1986 the International Marine Mammal Project organized a consumer boycott of tuna. The campaign urged U.S. tuna companies to end the practice of intentionally chasing and netting dolphins—which are often found in close proximity to tuna—with purse seine nets. In 1988 biologist Samuel LaBudde went aboard a Panamanian tuna fishing vessel and videotaped horrifying images of hundreds of dolphins dying in tuna nets. People around the world joined in the tuna boycott after seeing the shocking video. In 1990 the three largest tuna companies in the world—StarKist, Bumblebee, and Chicken of the Sea—agreed to discontinue purchasing, processing, and selling tuna caught with purse seine nets. Moreover, that same year the U.S. Congress enacted the Dolphin Protection Consumer Information Act, which created a "dolphin-safe" tuna label to assist consumers in purchasing tuna.

Environmental organizations also use boycotts to encourage the public to make responsible seafood choices that will protect dwindling fish stocks. In February 1998, for example, SeaWeb, an ocean environmental group, launched the "Give Swordfish a Break" campaign, a one-year boycott of North Atlantic Swordfish. The purpose of the campaign was to raise awareness about the problem of overfishing by using the swordfish as a symbol. According to SeaWeb Executive Director Vikki Spruill, boycotts "give consumers a voice in this issue."

Some fishery management experts claim, however, that boycotts are sometimes misguided. Thor Lassen, president of Ocean Trust, a nonprofit foundation dedicated to protecting ocean resources, claims that boycotts misrepresent the problem. For example, Lassen maintains, other swordfish species such as those in the South Atlantic and the Pacific appear to be healthy. Media reports, he claims, rarely make these distinctions, which gives the public the impression that the swordfish population is crashing worldwide. "Overall globally, overfishing has not been decreasing, nor has it been increasing," he says. "The condition of our fisheries in general has stabilized." Moreover, argues Rebecca Lent, director of the National Marine Fisheries Service (NMFS) Highly Migratory Species Division, "swordfish are not considered endangered."

Other commentators believe that because boycotts are not always based on accurate information, they often abuse the public's desire to help. Keith Keogh, president of the California Culinary Academy and a member of Ocean Trust's board, maintains that often the public has no patience for methodical deliberation when it comes to environmental issues. "In a lot of cases, people get very emotionally involved and jump on one bandwagon or another," he says. "The only way that you can stabilize emotion is with fact, and it takes a lot longer to develop facts and documentation than it does to develop emotion." For some activists such as SeaWeb's Spruill, however, generating emotion inspires action.

Whether or not boycotts are an appropriate conservation practice remains controversial. The authors of the viewpoints in the following chapter examine several other ocean management and conservation practices and debate their effectiveness.

"The numerous loopholes and exemptions in current environmental regulations give the cruise industry a 'license' to pollute."

Increased Regulation of Cruise Ship Waste Is Necessary

Kira Schmidt

The cruise ship industry's growing fleet is producing massive quantities of waste, claims Kira Schmidt in the following viewpoint. Unfortunately, she argues, pollution regulation has not kept pace with this growth and must be increased to control cruise ship waste. For example, she contends that the Clean Water Act does not prohibit the discharge of cruise ship graywater—water often contaminated with toxic cleaners, grease, and pesticides. Because the cruise ship industry has a history of violating existing marine pollution laws, Schmidt argues, more oversight is necessary. Schmidt is the director of Bluewater Network's Cruise Ship Campaign, which is working to strengthen environmental laws affecting the cruise ship industry.

As you read, consider the following questions:

1. According to Schmidt, how much waste can a typical cruise ship produce during a one-week voyage?
2. How did Royal Caribbean Cruises get away with dumping waste in violation of U.S. pollution laws, in the author's view?
3. Why does Schmidt believe voluntary efforts by the cruise industry are insufficient to ensure that cruise ship pollution of the marine environment will abate?

Kira Schmidt, "Criminal Cruise Ships: Soiling the Seven Seas," *Earth Island Journal*, vol. 15, Fall 2000. Copyright © 2000 by *Earth Island Journal*. Reproduced by permission.

The cruise ship industry has been riding a tidal wave of prosperity in recent years, with more than $1.5 billion in profits and an explosive growth rate of eight percent per year. There is no sign this tide is ebbing: By the end of 2004, the cruise industry plans to introduce 47 new ships to the North American fleet, up from today's 144.

Although the industry's continued success ultimately depends on the beauty of the oceans, the armada of cruise ships now plying the planet's waters trails behind it a wake of pollution. Today's cruise ships, the largest of which can carry more than 5,000 passengers and crew, are floating cities that generate titanic volumes of waste. A typical cruise ship on a one-week voyage produces approximately eight tons of garbage, as well as one million gallons of "graywater" (wastewater from sinks, showers, galleys and laundry), 210,000 gallons of sewage, and 25,000 gallons of oil-contaminated water. In addition, untold amounts of hazardous waste are generated on board from onboard printing, photo processing and dry cleaning operations.

A License to Pollute

Unfortunately, the environmental laws and regulations designed to control pollution from these colossal ships have not kept pace with the industry's runaway growth. The Clean Water Act was formulated before the dawn of the mega-cruise ship, when waste from vessels was not perceived as a significant problem. As a result, the numerous loopholes and exemptions in current environmental regulations give the cruise industry a "license" to pollute.

For example, the Clean Water Act makes it unlawful to discharge pollutants from any "point source" into US waters without a permit. But discharges of sewage and graywater from vessels are exempt from this requirement. Graywater—which, although not raw sewage ("blackwater"), often contains contaminants such as detergents, cleaners, oil, grease, metals and pesticides—can legally be dumped anywhere, even though the US Environmental Protection Agency (EPA) has found that graywater has the potential to cause adverse environmental effects.

The cruise industry has a history of illegally polluting the waters in which it sails. From 1993 to 1998, cruise ships were held responsible for 104 confirmed cases of illegal discharge of oil, garbage, and hazardous wastes, and required to pay more than $30 million in fines. This is just the tip of the trashberg. In reality, this number represents only a fraction of the industry's total illegal dumping. Several of these cases involved multiple incidents of illegal dumping that, according to the Department of Justice, numbered in the hundreds over the six-year period. Furthermore, this reflects only the quantity of detected cases; a recent report by the US General Accounting Office (GAO) reveals that the US Coast Guard's ability to detect and enforce marine pollution violations is hamstrung by numerous shortcomings.

Cruise Ships vs. Municipal Waste Production

Waste Source	Constituents	Produced per Day
Black Water miles (nautical)	Human waste	<16,000g
Gray Water (Cruise Ship)	Showers, sinks, laundry, other	<325,000g
Bilge Water (Cruise Ship)	Oily waste	<5,300g
Total		346,300g
Haines, Alaska	All of the above	307,000g

Ocean Conservancy, *Cruise Control*, May 2002.

In a particularly egregious case, Royal Caribbean Cruises, Ltd. (RCC) admitted routinely dumping waste oil from its ships and deliberately dumping hazardous photo processing, dry cleaning and print shop chemicals into US harbors and off-coast areas over a period of several years. RCC ships were rigged with secret piping systems designed to bypass pollution treatment equipment. The company's violations were characterized by investigators as so unscrupulous that they amounted to a "fleet-wide conspiracy [to] use our nation's waterways as its dumping ground," and so pervasive that criminal conduct was carried out as a routine business practice. Royal Caribbean finally signed a plea agreement in

July 1999, admitting guilt to a total of 21 felony counts in six US jurisdictions, and agreeing to pay a record $18 million in criminal fines.

In response to the cruise industry's flagrant and repeated violations of marine pollution laws, Bluewater Network has launched a national campaign to get the industry to clean up its act. Bluewater has filed a petition with the EPA [on March 17, 2000], highlighting the loopholes and exemptions in our environmental laws that let the cruise industry slip through the regulatory cracks. Bluewater is calling on the EPA to come up with ways to better monitor and regulate the cruise ship industry. Fifty-four other environmental organizations signed the petition, strengthening our call for action from the EPA to rein in the renegade cruise industry.

The EPA sat up and took notice: Within a month of receiving the petition, it formed an interagency work group to implement a rapid and coordinated response to the petition. The agency produced a whitepaper and held public hearings [in the summer of 2000], as first steps toward making recommendations regarding national cruiseship policies. The EPA also may issue an Advance Notice for Proposed Rulemaking on the regulation of cruise ship wastewater by the end of 2000. [The EPA held a hearing but did not issue the Advance Notice.]

Voluntary Efforts Are Not Enough

Not surprisingly, the cruise industry's reaction was less positive. Its representatives sent a letter to the EPA, Coast Guard and Department of Justice officials, members of Congress, and the 54 signatory organizations, denouncing the petition. The letter mocked the petition's tone and characterized its recommendations as unproductive and sensationalistic, claiming the cruise industry "cares about the environment and is proactively developing solutions to environmental challenges."

Although voluntary efforts by the cruise industry to clean up its act are steps in the right direction, they are insufficient to ensure that cruise ship pollution of the marine environment will abate. This industry has demonstrated that it cannot be trusted to protect the environment on its own. Furthermore, the industry's initiatives do not provide for active involvement by concerned citizens and organizations, and are not legally binding. It is clear that regulatory measures are needed to obligate the industry to closely monitor and control the tremendous volume of waste generated by their enormous ships.

In addition to the EPA's commendably rapid and well-coordinated response to Bluewater's petition, legislative action is being taken at the state level to tighten the screws on cruise ships. Bluewater has successfully lobbied lawmakers in Alaska and California to introduce bills that would require cruise ships to monitor and report regularly to the state environmental agency on all pollutants discharged into state waters and all wastes offloaded at ports.[1]

Now that policymakers have been made aware of the massive weight of the cruise ship pollution problem, there is hope that this human-cargo industry will finally receive the scrutiny and regulations it needs—and our threatened seas the protection they also require and deserve.

1. Alaska enacted legislation in 2001 that strengthened water quality protections. California has established a task force, but as of this writing, has enacted no laws.

"The cruise industry has proactively established guidelines regarding environmental practices . . . [that] meet or exceed all requirements of the law in the United States."

Voluntary Efforts to Control Cruise Ship Waste Are Adequate

Ted Thompson

In the following viewpoint Ted Thompson, executive vice president of the International Council of Cruise Lines (ICCL), claims that the ICCL has voluntarily established strict waste management practices and procedures that mirror or exceed federal legislation. According to Thompson, the cruise ship industry cares about the marine environment and works with lawmakers to prevent pollution. The cruise ship industry has a vested interest in protecting the beauty of the seas upon which it depends and is therefore a responsible environmental steward, Thompson maintains.

As you read, consider the following questions:

1. What perception does Thompson claim is damaging to the image and business prospects of the cruise industry?
2. According to Thompson, what does an analysis of the graywater dispersed by the typical cruise ship demonstrate?
3. Why does the cruise industry support legislation that restricts operations and provides harsh penalties, in the author's view?

Ted Thompson, "Presentation by the International Council of Cruise Lines at the Public Information Hearings of the Environmental Protection Agency Regarding Discharges from Cruise Ships," www.iccl.org, September 7, 2000. Copyright © 2000 by Ted Thompson. Reproduced by permission.

The International Council of Cruise Lines (ICCL) is an Arlington, Virginia, based trade association comprised of 16 member lines that carry approximately 85% of North American passengers on overnight international pleasure voyages. Several of our members are the dominant companies in the Alaskan market. Several operate ships in California and almost all operate vessels in the Caribbean market originating from ports in the southeastern United States. Additionally, vessels operated by ICCL members call on over 300 ports around the globe. Ours is a truly international industry.

Meeting International Standards

ICCL member vessels are not U.S. flagged. However, while operating in U.S. waters all U.S. environmental laws must be complied with. Additionally, all of our members must meet international regulations for both environmental protection and safety of life at sea at all times. To those of you who are familiar with SOLAS (the International Convention for the Safety of Life at Sea), MARPOL (the International Convention for the Prevention of Pollution from Ships), ISM (the International Safety Management Code), and STCW (the International Convention on Standards of Training, Certification and Watchkeeping for Seafarers), you know that these protocols set the benchmark for environmental and safety standards throughout the world. In fact, these international conventions to which the United States is signatory, have been adopted into the fabric of the U.S. maritime regulatory system.

As a business that is dependent on carrying passengers to beautiful locations where our passengers can experience nature's bounty, our membership recognizes that even a perception that the industry is not meeting U.S. or international standards is damaging to our image and therefore our business prospects. With this reality in mind, the cruise industry has proactively established guidelines regarding environmental practices, crime reporting, gaming, safety, labor practices, and medical treatment that each of the lines has agreed it will adhere to. These voluntary industry guidelines meet or exceed all requirements of the law in the United States.

Waste Management Practices and Procedures

Worthy of note here is the Cruise Industry Waste Management Practices and Procedures document agreed to by ICCL members in 1999. This policy document was unanimously adopted by the ICCL membership in November 1999, and has been incorporated into all of our member lines operating policies. In the development of these industry environmental management practices, the members of the International Council of Cruise Lines have endorsed policy goals based upon the following fundamental principles:

- Fully comply with applicable laws and regulations
- Maintain cooperative relationships with the regulatory community
- Design ships to be environmentally friendly
- Embrace new technology
- Conserve resources through purchasing strategies and product management
- Minimize waste generated and maximize reuse and recycling
- Optimize energy efficiency through conservation and management
- Manage water discharges
- Educate staff, guests and the community.

The Cruise Industry Waste Management Practices and Procedures document forms the basis for a Memorandum of Understanding between the State of Florida and our sister association, the Florida Caribbean Cruise Association, and has been utilized in discussions with federal agencies such as the Coast Guard and the EPA [Environmental Protection Agency] as well as the Alaska DEC [Department of Environmental Conservation] and legislators in Washington, Alaska and California. As technology develops, we will adopt additional self-imposed environmental standards that will be incorporated into this living document. . . .

In keeping with our commitment to seek out and incorporate new technologies, several ICCL members have committed approximately $1,000,000 apiece to field testing graywater treatment systems. These test systems, when fully developed and proven, are expected to remove sediments and impurities from graywater streams to the point that the output is essentially clean water. This clean water may then be reused or discharged without fear of any environmental impact.

The Impact of Graywater

In response to the question of what impact graywater and treated blackwater discharge has on the environment, and in an attempt to be proactive in addressing this issue, ICCL contracted a study by M. Rosenblatt & Sons to evaluate the dispersion of the waste water and any suspended solids and entrained substances into the sea as it is discharged. . . .

In the analysis, cruise ship graywater was characterized with respect to volume, flow rates, release frequencies, discharge durations, and locale. The constituents of graywater and the concentrations of these constituents to be expected at the discharge point were also defined. Based on an understanding of the mixing and volumetric dilution effects in the wake of a transiting vessel, the potential of graywater to adversely affect the environment in which cruise ships operate was assessed. The analysis was based on a 3000-person (combined passenger and crew) cruise ship generating 4200 m^3 [meters cubed] of graywater over a 7-day cruise period. The graywater discharge practices of such a ship, including the voluntary policy practices in effect for the Summer 2000 season, were considered.

As the extensive dilution calculations show, discharge constituents are diluted by a factor of approximately 1.93×10^{-5} (44,400) when a ship is moving at 4 knots. This dilution factor improves to about 7.71×10^{-6} (111,000) at 10 knots. These dilution factors are based strictly on the initial mixing concepts associated with the mixing zone and do not take into consideration the additional dispersion effects afforded by vessel wake, tidal, and current actions. The additional dispersion as a result of these factors may be as much as 3 to 5 orders of magnitude (1000 to 100,000 times more dispersion).

Within the confines of the available data and the assumptions made, ICCL believes that the analysis demonstrates that graywater dispersed constituent concentrations generated by the typical cruise ship are very low. This study provides a strong indication that the concentration of diluted constituents will be well below specified water quality criteria.

Recognizing that recent results from waste stream effluent testing exceed some of the parameters assumed in the
study, ICCL is redoing these calculations using the actual
test results where they are more conservative.

Providing Environmental Leadership

In June 2001, the International Council of Cruise Lines
(ICCL) and its members adopted a set of practices and procedures entitled *Cruise Industry Waste Management Practices
and Procedures*. These practices primarily build on the regulations of the International Maritime Organization and the
United States Environmental Protection Agency.

The three major cruise companies (Carnival Corporation,
Royal Caribbean Cruises Ltd. and P&O Princess Cruises plc)
and some smaller companies, such as Radisson Seven Seas
Cruises, have corporate programs for implementing the
ICCL practices and procedures, and, in some cases, exceeding these standards. All three major lines have programs that
include environmental awareness training for their crews,
screening of vendors who handle shore-side off-loading of
wastes and testing of technologies to minimize or eliminate
waste. Each of these programs is continually evolving to integrate the latest technologies and management practices.

James E.N. Sweeting and Scott L. Wayne, "A Shifting Tide: Environmental Challenges and Cruise Industry Responses," Center for Environmental
Leadership in Business, 2003.

We are also discussing an actual water-sampling program
with the EPA and the U.S. Coast Guard. Such an undertak-
ing would take and laboratory test water samples from identified water locations both before and after a cruise ship (or
ships) pass through while discharging graywater and treated
blackwater. It is expected that this water-sampling program
will yield definitive results that may be used for evaluating
the actual effect of cruise ship wastewater discharge.

Supporting Federal Legislation

[In] December [1999], federal legislation was introduced
that will establish mechanisms where by the American public could be assured that the cruise industry is indeed operating its vessels in the manner that the industry has stated.
[The amendment to the Clean Water Act passed on December 20, 2000.] The membership of the ICCL pledged its co-

operation with this effort. This landmark legislation would, in general:

1. Within specified waters, require cruise ships:
   - Not discharge untreated sewage (blackwater).
   - To discharge treated sewage only while the vessel is underway and proceeding at no less than 4 knots.
   - To discharge graywater (water from showers, sinks and galleys) only while the vessel is underway and proceeding at no less than 4 knots and if the vessel's graywater system is tested periodically to determine that the graywater does not contain chemicals used in the vessel's operation.
2. Permit relevant federal agencies concerned to promulgate additional regulation regarding the discharge of the above substances if they base additional regulations on relevant peer-reviewed scientific studies.
3. Enhance the Coast Guard's inspection authority over cruise ships.
4. Establish civil and criminal penalties for violating the operating restrictions outlined above.

The cruise industry agreed to and supported this legislation singling out our vessels for these very significant operating restrictions and penalties because this legislation merely codifies our current voluntary operating practices in Alaska. Indeed, when ICCL members adopt an industry policy such as to discharge graywater and treated blackwater only while a vessel is underway at a speed of 6 knots, this commitment applies to ship operations around the globe, not just in Alaska, or California or Florida.

We welcome the opportunity to publicly demonstrate that we are adhering to these practices, and that our industry is responsible and cares about the environment. We know of no other segment of maritime industry that will be willing or able to meet these types of standards.

In March [2000], the EPA in response to a petition from a number of environmental groups developed an action plan to evaluate cruise ship discharges as well as the industry's environmental operating practices. Indeed, these public meetings are a part of the EPA evaluation process. We have met with EPA officials on several occasions. [In late August 2000], in

Yorktown, Virginia, together with the U.S. Coast Guard, ICCL co-hosted a two-day workshop for EPA, other Federal officials, other cruise industry segments and public environmental advocacy groups. This forum focused on the practical application of the international regulatory regime and other aspects of environmental management practices adopted by ICCL vessel operators. . . .

The International Council of Cruise Lines together with its sister associations, the North West CruiseShip Association (NWCA) and the Florida Caribbean Cruise Association (FCCA) and the cruise vessel operators of each of these associations are dedicated to responsible environmental management and protection of our natural resources. We are committed to working in partnership with the Environmental Protection Agency, the United States Coast Guard, other federal and state environmental protection agencies and public environmental advocacy groups such as the Centers for Marine Conservation, Ocean Advocates and the Bluewater Network to find productive solutions to the very real issues that confront us on a daily basis.

"Should the increasing CO_2 content of the atmosphere be determined to have adverse impacts much worse than their advantages, the further demonstration of . . . [ocean fertilization] can provide a solution."

Ocean Fertilization Can Reduce Global Warming

Michael Markels and Richard T. Barber

Global warming, which many experts believe is caused by an increase in carbon dioxide (CO_2) in the atmosphere resulting from the burning of fossil fuels, has generated worries that ocean levels will rise and weather patterns will change. In response, many international treaties have been developed that call for nations to reduce production of CO_2. However, fertilizing the ocean with iron to remove CO_2 from the atmosphere is more economical than trying to reduce CO_2 emissions, argue Michael Markels and Richard T. Barber in the following viewpoint. The authors claim that adding iron to encourage marine plant growth will reduce atmospheric levels of CO_2. Markels is the founder of GreenSea Venture, Inc., an ocean farming company. Barber is a professor of biological oceanography at Duke University.

As you read, consider the following questions:
1. What are the adverse economic effects of current attempts to reduce CO_2 emissions, in the authors' view?
2. According to the authors, what is the disadvantage of injecting CO_2 into coal seams or pumping it to the ocean floor?

The CO_2 content of the atmosphere has increased from about 280 ppm [parts per million] to about 362 ppm during the last 60 years. During the 1980's the rate of increase of CO_2 in the atmosphere, in terms of carbon metric tons, was about 3.3 gigatons of carbon per year (GtC/yr). Fossil fuel emissions were about 5.5 GtC/yr (20 Gt CO_2/yr) and terrestrial emissions were about 1.1 GtC/yr during that period, so about 3.3 GtC/yr, 60% of fossil fuel emissions, were sequestered naturally. Of this, about 2.0 GtC/yr was absorbed by the oceans and 1.3 GtC/yr by the land. The remaining 40%, 2.2 GtC (8.1 $GtCO_2$)/yr, contributed to the increasing atmospheric CO_2 concentration. This increase in the CO_2 content of the atmosphere has led to concerns that this increase will result in global climate change, which, over time, can have adverse effects on weather, sea level and human survival. This concern has led to the 1992 Rio Treaty, the IPCC [Intergovernmental Panel on Climate Change] Working Group and the Kyoto Protocol of 1997, which call for a reduction of emissions of 34% by 2050 and a reduction of 70% from the then-expected emissions from the industrial nations by 2100. These reductions, if put into effect, would have serious adverse effects on the economy of the United States, causing loss of jobs, decrease in our standard of living and a reduction in the life span of our citizens. These required reductions would not address the concerns that demand an approach to permit the reversal of atmospheric CO_2 increase, should this become necessary.

The Problem of Increased CO_2

What is the basis for peoples' concerns? Part is the fear of the new and unknown. Any change that is not purposeful may be viewed with apprehension. "It is probably bad unless I can control it." The other part is the unknown aspects of the science. While the results of increased CO_2 in the atmosphere have generally been benign so far there is genuine concern that at some point the atmosphere may become unstable and the oceans may freeze, the atmosphere may lose its water to outer space or the earth may become so hot that the atmosphere may become mostly water vapor. Here too, the key is to have available a technology that can be applied to the problem if required, to reverse the increased CO_2 content of the atmosphere at a cost that people are prepared to bear.

The current approach to the problem of atmospheric CO_2 increase is to take specific actions now to reduce the risk of adverse consequences in the future. These actions are to increase the efficiency of energy production and use and to change our standard of living to reduce our dependence on energy in our lives. Energy efficiency can often be increased, but we have been doing this for over 200 years, so there is not a lot of gain remaining before we run into thermodynamic barriers. Even at 100% efficiency we still add CO_2 to the atmosphere, so this can never address peoples' concerns. We can also address the other side of the problem, which is to increase the rate at which CO_2 is removed from the atmosphere. If we could increase this enough we could bring the *net* increase in CO_2 emissions to zero, providing a solution to the problem of peoples' concerns. The availability of this solution will permit us to avoid precipitous actions and await the proven requirement to take steps to lower the atmospheric CO_2 level as may be prudent.

Removing CO_2 from the Atmosphere

CO_2 is removed from the atmosphere by plants using the Sun's energy to convert it to biomass. This biomass may be used as food by bacteria, fungi and animals that obtain energy by reacting it with oxygen from the air and respiring CO_2 back to the atmosphere. Over time, a portion of the biomass formed has been sequestered in the earth and in the ocean bottom, forming fossil fuels that we burn to obtain energy to support our standard of living. Numerous projects have been undertaken to increase tree growth in the tropics. These projects suffer from a short lifetime, generally 20 to 50 years, and the difficulty of assuring that forest fires, poaching, etc., will not result in an early recycling of the carbon to the atmosphere. Other CO_2 sequestering technologies have been proposed, including injection of liquid CO_2 into geological formations or into the deep ocean.

The injection of CO_2 into coal seams and natural gas producing formations to increase methane production has been well proven and is commercially viable where relatively pure

CO_2 is available. This is the case where natural gas wells produce a mix of CO_2 and methane, which is separated leaving a CO_2-rich stream at no additional cost. These CO_2-rich streams can also be disposed of in deep saline aquifers such as is being done in the North Sea. The capacity of these alternatives is low since not much pure CO_2 is available near disposal sites. A larger capacity alternative is to separate the CO_2 from flue gas at electric power plants, liquefy and transport it to a location where it can be transferred to a ship for transport to the deep ocean. There, the ship will lower a two-mile long injection pipe and pump the liquid CO_2 to the ocean floor. Each of these steps is expensive and energy intensive, with the result that the approach is expected to cost in the range of $300 per ton of carbon or $80 per ton of CO_2 sequestered.

There are environmental concerns since we would be adding a new chemical to the ocean floor, liquid CO_2, which may produce hydrates and other chemicals over time. Liquid fuels used for transportation are also difficult to burn so as to capture the CO_2 produced. While increased efficiency is usually advantageous it still results in CO_2 release to the atmosphere. This, again, indicates that sequestration of the CO_2 is likely to be the best approach.

Fertilizing the Ocean

The best approach is to sequester CO_2 in the deep ocean by causing a bloom of plant life that then sinks to the deep waters where it remains for about 1600 years, as measured by the ^{14}C to ^{12}C ratio [the normal ratio of these two isotopes as found in atmospheric CO_2] of upwelling of deep ocean water off of Peru. This process is possible because large areas of the oceans have excess, unused plant nutrients and much less than expected phytoplankton biomass, the so-called HNLC [high nutrient, low chlorophyll] waters. The difference is that the HNLC waters are deficient in one or more of the micronutrients required for plants to grow. While several essential metals may be involved in the limitation of growth in HNLC areas, iron has been shown to be the major micronutrient. Generally, 100,000 moles of carbon biomass require 16,000 moles of fixed nitrogen, 1,000 moles of soluble phosphorous and one mole of available iron. The main difficulty is the iron. Since surface ocean waters are highly oxygenated, any soluble iron is converted to Fe^{+++} with a half-life of about one hour and precipitates as $Fe(OH)_3$. A shovel full of earth is about 5.6% iron on the average. The ocean, on the other hand, has 0.0000000001 or less moles per liter of iron, too little to sustain plant growth. The first problem, then, is how to add iron to the ocean so that it will be available to the phytoplankton (plants). The phytoplankton themselves exude organic chelating compounds into the ocean that protect some of the iron that is there from precipitation. Adding iron in the form of a chelate so that it does not precipitate but remains available for plant fertilization can mimic this natural process. An essential element that may be in short supply in nutrient-depleted, tropical ocean waters is phosphorous. Most phosphates are soluble and can be added directly to the ocean. Since the phosphate may attack the iron chelate, it may be necessary to keep the concentrations of both fertilizers low. This can be done by adding them to the ocean separately in the form of small floating pellets that release the fertilizing element slowly over a period of days. This process has been tested by GreenSea Venture, Inc. (GSV) in the Gulf of Mexico with good results. The remaining required essential element is fixed nitrogen. Bluegreen algae or, as they are more properly called, cyanobacteria, have the ability to fix nitrogen, so inducing a bloom of nitrogen fixers might supply this requirement.

Sequestering CO_2

When the fertilizer mixed with water is added to the tropical ocean surface it mixes rapidly in the warm waters (the mixed layer) and starts the phytoplankton bloom. The plants, mostly diatoms, multiply rapidly, increasing their numbers by two to three times per day, until they run out of one of the required nutrients. They then cease growing, lose the ability to maintain buoyancy and sink through the thermocline at a rate of about 75 feet a day. The sinking biomass is trapped in the cold, dense waters where it is eaten by animal life and bacteria. This slowly converts the biomass back to CO_2 in the deep waters. Where high concentrations of biomass are generated and reach the ocean floor they may be covered by mud and debris, leading to anoxic digestion. The methane produced is converted to methane hydrates by the high pressure of the deep ocean. It has been estimated that there is twice as much carbon in the methane hydrates of the deep ocean floor than all the terrestrial fossil fuels combined. It is worth noting that the addition of CO_2 in this low concentration, natural process is not expected to have any adverse environmental impact on the ocean, which now has about 85 times as much dissolved inorganic carbon as the atmosphere.

Iron Fertilization Is a Truly New Concept

The fundamental concept that iron controls the growth of phytoplankton in much of the world's oceans was formally postulated with supporting data in the late 1980's. During the 1990's and into 2002, a series of experiments, ranging from bench-scale assays to large-scale fertilizations of 100-square kilometer patches of ocean from the North Pacific to Antarctica, have been conducted to test the "iron hypothesis" and the results of these experiments have confirmed the initial hypothesis.

GreenSea Venture, "Development of Iron Fertilization Science," 2002.

Since our objective is to sequester CO_2 to the deep ocean it is important that we minimize the proportion of the biomass produced that is processed by animal life and bacteria in the mixing layer above the thermocline. This can be done by fertilizing in pulses, so that the slower-growing animal life cannot multiply effectively before the diatoms have bloomed, died and gone below the thermocline, a period of less than 20 days. The fraction of the biomass produced that is sequestered below the thermocline has been measured. It depends principally on the amount of animal life available to eat the biomass and convert it back into CO_2 in the highly oxygenated surface waters. Where the ecosystem is in balance with large amounts of animal life the sequestered carbon is about 10% of primary production and consists mainly of animal parts, scales, bones and fecal pellets. Where animal life is absent the ratio may go as high as 80% sequestered. Measurements made in the tropical Pacific Ocean off of Peru produced a ratio of 53% sequestered beneath the thermocline. We have used this measurement in our calculations. We must also test the waters we intend to fertilize in order to add the correct amount and mix to produce the optimum result. To achieve this we select the waters for fertilization to include a strong, shallow thermocline, tropical sunshine and high nutrient, low chlorophyll (HNLC) conditions. These waters can be found in the tropical Pacific near the equator west of the Galapagos Islands. The cool wind-driven currents go directly to the west before reaching the Line Islands of Polynesia. The 3,000,000 square miles of these HNLC waters can sequester about 0.4 $GtCO_2$/yr. Recent studies have shown that, because of the rapidly growing forests and verdant agriculture, North America has an uptake of 1.7 $GtCO_2$/yr and an emission of 1.6 $GtCO_2$/yr. While this rough balance is variable, depending on weather-stimulated growth it illustrates that sequestering capability such as that of the Pacific Equatorial Current can be significant in affecting the C content of the atmosphere. . . .

The Commercialization of CO_2 Sequestration

Should the increasing CO_2 content of the atmosphere be determined to have adverse impacts much worse than their advantages, the further demonstration of this technology can provide a solution, relieving the concerns regarding the continuous increase of these adverse net impacts. CO_2 sequestering could then be carried out in the equatorial Pacific and in other HNLC waters, especially off of Antarctica, the main areas of the oceans that have a high capacity of sequestering CO_2. For instance, if all the CO_2 in the atmosphere were sequestered in the ocean, it would raise the average concentration of CO_2 in the ocean by only about 1.2%. The ocean chemistry would not be altered significantly and the increase in outgassing of the CO_2 from the ocean surface would be minimal.

The cost of sequestering CO_2 on a commercial scale is expected to be about $1.00 per ton of CO_2. The sales price for CO_2 sequestering credits, should they become tradable, would be about $2.00 per ton of CO_2, to include the cost of verification, overhead and profit. It is expected that these credits would be highly valued since they would not suffer from the problems of fire hazard, leakage and additionality the forest projects for CO_2 sequestering face. Such credits could be produced within a few years of a successful technology demonstration. Alternately, technology development could be continued with the objective of eventual large-scale CO_2 sequestration to address major climate perturbations.

Creating New Choices

The expected impacts of a successful demonstration of the technology and the measurement of significant sequestration response by the ocean to the planned chelated iron addition could be significant. The costly early actions now being contemplated to counteract possible future impacts of increased CO_2 content of the atmosphere would no longer be needed and instead all responses could be tied to measured consequences, which could then be reversed. This would open new options, avoid the unnecessary use of scarce resources and refocus attention on actual problems rather than seeking to deal with possible future scenarios. Many entities, both governmental and industrial may decide to do very useful things based on these concerns, such as improved energy efficiency and the exploration of new energy resources. This is to the good of society where they make economic sense and should be implemented in any case.

A CO_2 credit system may be instituted that will allow trading of credits to generate the lowest cost. Credits from sequestering CO_2 in the oceans should be a part of this effort so as to take early advantage of this lower cost, environmentally benign, low human impact and robust capacity approach to solving the global warming concerns, should this become necessary.

Many approaches for dealing with the increase in the CO_2 content of the atmosphere have been proposed, but sequestration by ocean fertilization has received little attention. It is new, far away and poorly understood by many. The initial reaction is that not enough is known to warrant attention at this time. While this reaction may have had merit in the past, the last few years have seen a great increase in knowledge about the oceans, especially the equatorial Pacific, where moored and floating buoy systems, research vessel voyages and continuous satellite monitoring have all greatly increased our knowledge and understanding. The last remaining piece of the puzzle is to quantify the response of this HNLC ocean water to iron fertilization . . . which can lead to solving the problem of peoples' concerns rather than just working on it, thereby saving time and costs while greatly reducing the risk of adverse consequences.

"The known consequences and uncertainties of ocean fertilization already far outweigh hypothetical benefits."

Ocean Fertilization Will Harm the World's Oceans

Sallie W. Chisholm, Paul G. Falkowski, and John J. Cullen

Many experts fear that global warming, which some believe is caused by an increase in carbon dioxide (CO_2) in the atmosphere resulting from the burning of fossil fuels, will increase ocean levels and alter weather patterns. Since CO_2 is removed from the atmosphere by plants during photosynthesis, some researchers theorize that fertilizing the ocean with iron to increase CO_2 consuming marine plants will reduce CO_2 levels in the atmosphere. This hypothesis is unproven, claim Sallie W. Chisholm, Paul G. Falkowski, and John J. Cullen in the following viewpoint. In fact, the authors argue, ocean fertilization could permanently and adversely alter the marine ecology by artificially increasing the amount of phytoplankton in the oceans. Chisholm is an engineering professor at the Massachusetts Institute of Technology, Falkowski is a geology professor at Rutgers University, and Cullen is an oceanography professor at Dalhousie University in Canada.

As you read, consider the following questions:
1. According to the authors, what happened as a result of press coverage of ocean fertilization experiments?
2. What do most models predict will be the likely result of sustained fertilization, in the authors' view?

Sallie W. Chisholm, Paul G. Falkowski, and John J. Cullen, "Dis-Crediting Ocean Fertilization," *Science*, www.sciencemag.org, vol. 294, October 12, 2001, pp. 309–10. Copyright © 2001 by the American Association for the Advancement of Science. Reproduced by permission.

The oceans play a key role in the global carbon cycle and climate regulation. Central to this function are phytoplankton, single-celled photosynthetic organisms that convert CO_2 [carbon dioxide] to organic carbon in the surface oceans. Although accounting for <1% of photosynthetic biomass, phytoplankton are responsible for roughly half of the carbon fixation on Earth. The organic carbon they produce is mostly eaten by other organisms in the surface waters, and regenerated to CO_2 as these organisms respire. But some organic carbon sinks to the deep ocean, thus reducing CO_2 in the surface layer and elevating it in the deep sea.

An Interest in Carbon Sequestration

The CO_2 concentration gradient maintained by this "biological pump" removes CO_2 from the atmosphere by storing it in the ocean interior. Increased interest in carbon sequestration strategies for mitigating climate change—such as reforestation, CO_2 storage in geological formations, and direct injection of CO_2 into the deep ocean—has drawn attention to the biological pump. Some entrepreneurs speculate that if the oceans were fertilized, the rate of carbon flux to the deep sea could be increased, and the incremental carbon could be sold as credits in the developing global carbon marketplace.

If implemented on a large scale, ocean fertilization would, by design, change the ecology of the oceans. The potential long-term consequences of this purposeful eutrophication strategy are cause for great concern, yet the idea is gaining momentum. Here, we examine the validity of the concept, and propose a policy option that could protect Earth's largest ecosystem from this dangerous course.

The Iron Hypothesis

The biological pump has been the focus of major research programs for decades. For a long time, nitrogen (N) and phosphorus (P) were believed to limit the primary productivity that drives the pump. Yet in large areas in the subarctic northeast Pacific, the equatorial Pacific, and the Southern Ocean, N and P are never exhausted in surface waters, and phytoplankton biomass is less than expected. [John H.] Martin suggested that it is the scarcity of biologically available iron in these high-nutrient, low-chlorophyll (HNLC) regions that makes it impossible for the phytoplankton to use the excess N and P. He also recognized that atmospheric dust from land is an important source of iron for the sea and that HNLC regions receive a relatively small dust flux. Furthermore, he noted that ice core records of atmospheric CO_2 and dust concentrations over the past 180,000 years are anti-correlated: when dust was high, CO_2 was low. This is consistent with the notion that during the arid glacial periods, dust transport was greater, more iron was available, and the biological pump delivered more CO_2 to the deep sea. This "iron hypothesis," initially met with skepticism, has slowly garnered support from geochemists as one of several possible mechanisms that can account for changes in atmospheric CO_2 during glacial-interglacial transitions. The iron hypothesis was extended by Martin to imply that the deliberate addition of iron to the surface oceans could increase carbon storage in the deep sea. Only partly in jest he quipped: "Give me half a tanker of iron, and I will give you the next ice age."

Although at the time there was no direct evidence that iron limited primary production in HNLC regions, by the late 1980s the possibility of fertilizing the oceans with iron to mitigate the rise in atmospheric CO_2 was beginning to be taken seriously. This prompted the American Society of Limnology and Oceanography (ASLO) to issue a resolution discouraging iron fertilization as a policy option.

Conducting Iron Addition Experiments

Around the same time (sadly, just after Martin died), oceanographers began to pursue small-scale (ca. 100 km²), iron addition experiments in the open ocean. These experiments were designed to determine whether iron was indeed the limiting nutrient in HNLC regions, as Martin had hypothesized. They were not intended to demonstrate the feasibility of fertilization for purposes of carbon sequestration. Over the past 10 years, four such small-scale experiments have been conducted in the equatorial Pacific and the Southern Ocean. They have shown that adding small amounts of iron to these waters increases phytoplankton productivity and biomass over periods of a few days to weeks. In one experiment, phytoplankton biomass increased 20- to 30-fold.

These scientific experiments, which were conducted on very small scales, did not document a net transfer of CO_2 from the atmosphere to the deep sea. Press coverage, however, left the impression that phytoplankton hold the cure for global warming. Corporations and private entrepreneurs took note, and numerous patents were filed on ocean fertilization processes, anticipating a global market in which credits for carbon sequestered through fertilization might be traded.

One such enterprise, GreenSea Venture, Inc., has recruited leading oceanographers to join their mission, which includes a proposed 8000 km^2 demonstration experiment in the equatorial Pacific. Carbon-corp USA has also promoted ocean carbon sequestration through fertilization. They have described a process in which commercial ships that routinely traverse the high seas release small amounts of a proprietary fertilizer mix.

The Ocean Technology Group of the University of Sydney has patented an "ocean nourishment" process in which ammonia is produced from atmospheric N_2 and piped to coastal waters to stimulate phytoplankton blooms. In partnership with a Japanese firm, they have approached the Chilean government and the World Bank about installing such a facility in Chilean waters.

Despite the concerns of many oceanographers and environmental groups, the concept of industrial ocean fertilization is winning advocates. Proponents claim that ocean fertilization is an easily controlled, verifiable process that mimics nature; and that it is an environmentally benign, long-term solution to atmospheric CO_2 accumulation. These claims are, quite simply, not true.

The Problems with Ocean Fertilization

It is not easily controlled. A fertilized patch in turbulent ocean currents is not like a plot of land. The oceans are a fluid medium, beyond our control.

It does not mimic nature. The proponents argue that ocean fertilization is similar to the natural iron deposition from atmospheric dust, and to the natural upwelling of nutrients from the deep sea. These analogies are flawed. Phytoplankton species that bloom in response to upwelling are adapted to a turbulent regime, and a complex mixture of upwelled nutrients that are part of the natural nutrient regeneration cycle of the oceans. Furthermore, proposed designs employ an artificial chelator, lignin acid sulfonate, which is designed to keep iron in solution and is chemically different from atmospheric iron sources. Finally, in intensive commercial ocean fertilization, iron would be delivered to ecosystems at rates that do not mimic the 1000-year time scales of glacial transition periods.

Despite the claims of the proponents, carbon sequestration from ocean fertilization is not easily verified. Besides measuring carbon flux profiles and comparing them with a control basin, one would have to determine what fraction of the natural stores of N and P used up in the fertilized patch would no longer be available for phytoplankton growth in downstream ocean regions. This would require complex numerical models of large-scale ocean physics and biogeochemistry, the predictions of which cannot be validated through small perturbations such as patch fertilizations.

The proponents' claim that fertilization for carbon sequestration would be environmentally benign is inconsistent with almost everything we know about aquatic ecosystems. Fertilization changes the composition of the phytoplankton community; it is precisely this feature that gives it the potential for increasing carbon flux to the deep sea. Correspondingly, the oceans' food webs and biogeochemical cycles would be altered in unintended ways. We have learned this from inadvertent enrichment of lakes and coastal waters with nutrients from agricultural runoff, something we have been trying to reverse for decades.

Compromising the Oceans

Fertilization advocates try to counter these concerns by arguing that the oceans have already been compromised. Indeed, we have known for decades that human activities have resulted in depleted fisheries, coastal eutrophication, heavy metal accumulation, and rising dissolved CO_2 in the surface waters. But does this unintended deterioration justify large-scale, purposeful interference with ocean ecosystems? The oceans provide valuable ecosystem services for the maintenance of our planet and the sustenance of human society, and the carbon cycle is intimately coupled with those of other elements, some of which play critical roles in climate regulation. One cannot sequester additional carbon without changing coupled biogeochemical cycles.

Models predict, for example, that sustained fertilization would likely result in deep ocean hypoxia or anoxia. This would shift the microbial community toward organisms that produce greenhouse gases such as methane and nitrous oxide, with much higher warming potentials than CO_2. Some models predict that Southern Ocean fertilization would change patterns of primary productivity globally by reducing the availability of N and P in the Equatorial Pacific. The uncertainties surrounding these cumulative, long-term, consequences of fertilization cannot be reduced through short term, small-scale experiments.

Potential Consequences of Iron Fertilization

- Fertilization could lead to increases in undesirable or even toxic species of phytoplankton
- Toxic algal blooms could emerge and choke fish and other marine life populations
- Sinking decaying organic matter uses oxygen through respiration in deep waters
- This leads to the potential formation of anoxic zones ("dead zones") in the ocean
- Anoxic environments lead to the production of methane and nitrous oxide
- Methane has 21 times the harmful potential of CO_2; N_2O has 206 times the harmful potential of CO_2

Robb Stey and Brendan O'Donnell, "Ocean Iron Fertilization: A Global Warming Panacea?" December 7, 2000.

To us, the known consequences and uncertainties of ocean fertilization already far outweigh hypothetical benefits. Models predict that if all of the unused N and P in Southern Ocean surface waters were converted to organic carbon over the next 100 years (an unlikely extreme), 15% of the anthropogenic CO_2 could be hypothetically sequestered. Because deep ocean CO_2 reservoirs are eventually re-exposed to the atmosphere through global ocean circulation, this would not be a permanent solution. It is argued, however, that it would buy us time. Given both the certain and likely consequences of widespread ocean fertilization, which at some critical scale would not be reversible, we do not find this justification compelling.

The Risks of Commercialization

We are not arguing against selective small-scale iron enrichment experiments designed to answer questions about how ocean ecosystems function. Such experiments have proven to be extremely valuable scientifically and produce very transient effects. Our objections are to commercialized ocean fertilization—the scaled-up consequences of which could be very damaging to the global oceans.

To put ocean fertilization as a carbon sequestration option into perspective, we need to remind ourselves why CO_2 is increasing in the atmosphere at such a rapid rate and to ask how sequestration could mitigate this rise. Two basic carbon cycles operate on Earth. The first cycle is driven by volcanic outgassing of CO_2 coupled to the metamorphic weathering of silicate rocks. This cycle operates on time scales of millions of years. The second cycle involves the biological reduction of CO_2 to organic matter and the subsequent oxidation of the organic matter by respiration. A tiny fraction of organic carbon escapes respiratory oxidation and is incorporated into the lithosphere, forming fossil fuels. This process transfers carbon from the fast, biologically driven cycle to the slow, tectonically controlled cycle.

By burning fossil fuels, humans are bringing carbon from the slow cycle back into the atmosphere. The biological sinks—chiefly forests and phytoplankton—cannot adjust fast enough, and do not have the capacity to remove all this anthropogenic carbon from the atmosphere. For carbon sequestration to work as a climate mitigation strategy, CO_2 must be sequestered back into the slow carbon cycle. Ocean fertilization does not do so; nor does direct injection of CO_2 into mid-ocean waters, another proposed method for carbon sequestration. Direct injection short-circuits the biological pump but it may trigger unknown effects on deep sea life and thus on biogeochemical processes.

Given all of the risks and limitations, why has the idea of industrial scale ocean fertilization not been summarily dismissed? One answer lies in carbon trading. One need not fertilize entire ocean basins to sequester an amount of carbon that could yield commercial benefits on this anticipated market. If scientifically sound verification criteria could be developed, relatively small-scale fertilizations could be very profitable for individual entrepreneurs. True, no single application would cause sustained ecosystem damage. But if it is profitable for one, it would be profitable for many, and the cumulative effects of many such implementations would result in large-scale consequences—a classic "tragedy of the commons."

One simple way to avert this potential tragedy is to remove the profit incentive for manipulation of the ocean commons. We suggest that ocean fertilization, in the open seas or territorial waters, should never become eligible for carbon credits.

Periodical Bibliography

The following articles have been selected to supplement the diverse views presented in this chapter.

Tundi Agardy	"Creating Havens for Marine Life," *Issues in Science and Technology*, Fall 1999.
Helen Baulch	"Ironing Out Warming Wrinkles: Fertilizing the Oceans with Iron Could Help Block Climate Change—or It Could Make Things Worse," *Alternatives Journal*, Spring 1999.
Lydia K. Bergen and Mark H. Carr	"Establishing Marine Reserves: How Can Science Best Inform Policy?" *Environment*, March 2003.
P. Dee Boersma and Julia K. Parrish	"Limiting Abuse: Marine Protected Areas, a Limited Solution," *Ecological Economics*, 1999.
Sallie W. Chisholm	"Oceanography: Stirring Times in the Southern Ocean," *Nature*, October 5, 2000.
Gershon Cohen	"Cruise Ships Fail Pollution Tests," *Earth Island Journal*, Summer 2001.
Denis Faye	"Marine Protection: Learning to Give and Take," *Ecos*, January 1999.
General Accounting Office	"Marine Pollution: Progress Made to Reduce Marine Pollution by Cruise Ships, but Important Issues Remain," February 28, 2000. www.gao.gov.
Charles Graeber	"Dumping Iron," *Wired*, November 2000.
Kenneth S. Johnson and David M. Karl	"Is Ocean Fertilization Credible and Creditable?" *Science*, April 19, 2002.
David Malakoff	"Marine Ecology: Picturing the Perfect Preserve," *Science*, April 12, 2002.
Tom Neale	"No Discharge Zone: Problem or Solution?" *Cruising World*, May 1998.
Ocean Conservancy	"Cruise Control: How Cruise Ships Affect the Marine Environment," OceanConservancy.org, May 29, 2002.
Sean Paige	"NOAA's Disputed Archipelago," *Insight*, May 4, 1998.
Fred Pearce	"Blooming Marvelous," *New Scientist*, October 11, 2000.
Andrew C. Revkin	"Chefs Joining Boycott in Effort to Save Imperiled Sea Bass," *New York Times*, May 21, 2002.

Phyllis White and Robert White | "Leaving Less in the Wake," *Cruise Travel*, June 2001.

Robert J. Wilder, Mia J. Tegner, and Paul K. Dayton | "Saving Marine Biodiversity," *Issues in Science and Technology*, Spring 1999.

Jennifer Wolcott | "A Fish Story: Navigating Seafood Choices," *Christian Science Monitor*, November 13, 2002.

CHAPTER 3

What Strategies Would Best Promote Sustainable Fishing?

Chapter Preface

Many of those concerned about the oceans, from conservationists to fishers, have recommended strategies to promote sustainable fisheries. One proposed strategy is to ban the use of large bottom trawling gear that some analysts claim is destroying fisheries. Industry advocates argue, however, that these bans will economically devastate fishing communities without averting the damage that they are designed to prevent.

Bottom trawl nets are like enormous butterfly nets. The "footrope," the bottom edge at the mouth of the net, is usually made of heavy-gauge chain rigged with weights and rollers or rockhoppers. Rollers are steel or rubber tires or balls that rotate on the footrope as it drags across the ocean floor. Rollers, which can be from four to eighteen inches in diameter, reduce the amount of mud that the net collects. Because bottom trawlers using rollers could not get to fish where the habitat was rough without risking expensive damage to the nets, these trawlers were used primarily to harvest fish species that inhabited sandy or muddy areas.

In the 1980s, however, the fishing industry developed "rockhopper" nets with large, heavy wheels, between eight and thirty-two inches in diameter, that could roll over obstructions. Areas of the ocean floor once protected from bottom trawling gear are now pursued with vigor. Some conservationists claim that the larger equipment has damaged the ocean floor. Sediment is stirred up in massive clouds, and when it drifts back to the bottom, it can suffocate shellfish, corals, and sedentary seafloor life. Rockhoppers destroy fragile sea floor life such as sea anemones, sponges, and deep-sea coral. According to marine ecologist Carl Safina, "Bottom trawling is akin to harvesting corn with bulldozers that scoop up topsoil and cornstalks along with the ears."

Some experts claim that rockhopper trawlers are destroying the once protected habitat that serves as nurseries for commercially important fish and is also home to the fish these commercial fish eat. According to biologist Gerald Smith, "Those organisms not captured and killed in the bycatch of commercial trawling are physically scrambled and their habitat disturbed, with negative consequences to the food webs they anchor." Fish depletion first began at the top of the food web: The large fish, most prized by consumers, declined first, followed by smaller fish at lower levels of the food chain. The development of bottom trawling further added to the problem by destroying the food supply from the bottom up, which in Smith's view spells disaster for the marine environment and the fishing industry.

For some experts the solution is to ban large trawl gear. U.S. Representative Joel Hefley introduced a bill that would place size limits on ground gear used on bottom trawls and ban the use of rollers and rockhoppers that are more than eight inches in diameter. However, Justin Leblanc, vice president of the National Fisheries Institute, argues that an outright ban on large trawl gear could make matters worse. Although a general ban of large gear might prevent its use on the rough substrates the legislation seeks to protect, it would also prevent its use on the soft-bottom substrates. Fishers would be forced to return to using the smaller gear, which has a greater impact on soft-bottom areas, he maintains. Moreover, claims Leblanc, a return to small trawl gear might encourage creative modifications to the equipment that would allow fishers to fish in the rocky substrates; this modified trawling gear could have a more adverse impact on sensitive areas than large gear.

Fishers worry that these bans will devastate the trawler industry. According to Leblanc, "Alaska could lose $180 million worth of groundfish landing annually, the West Coast could lose $65 million worth of groundfish annually, and virtually the entire New England groundfish, shrimp, and whiting fisheries worth over $140 million annually could be lost." As of this writing, Hefley's bill remains in committee.

Whether or not large bottom trawl gear should be banned remains the subject of debate. The authors of the viewpoints in the following chapter examine additional strategies for protecting fish and debate their effectiveness to promote sustainable fisheries.

> "[Marine Protected Areas] represent the single most comprehensive, robust, and effective ocean management tool available."

Fully Protected Marine Reserves Will Promote Sustainable Fishing

David White

In order to sustain threatened fish populations and protect America's marine ecosystems, the nation must expand the number of Marine Protected Areas, especially "no-take" reserves that close ocean areas to fishing, claims David White in the following viewpoint, originally given as testimony before the President's Commission on Ocean Policy. Studies worldwide show that fish populations grow in no-take marine reserves and in adjacent ocean areas, White maintains. As a result, he contends, no-take reserves promote sustainable fishing in nearby waters. White is Southeastern Regional Director of the Ocean Conservancy.

As you read, consider the following questions:
1. In White's view, what is the value of having a full array of control areas when studying the marine environment?
2. According to the author, on what should the debate about marine protected areas focus?
3. To whom does White say the waters of the United States belong?

David White, testimony before the President's Commission on Ocean Policy, St. Petersburg, Florida, February 22, 2001.

Thank you for inviting me to speak before you today. My name is David White, and I am the Director of The Ocean Conservancy's Southeastern Regional Office, based here in St. Petersburg [Florida]. We cover marine conservation issues in the South Atlantic and Gulf Coast states, working in four main program areas: ecosystem protection, clean oceans, and fish and marine wildlife conservation. The Ocean Conservancy has over 900,000 members and volunteers, with over 10,000 members and 32,000 volunteers here in Florida alone.

I would like to focus my comments on the need to develop an adequate network of marine protected areas—MPAs—in America's oceans. But before I begin, please allow me to define my terms. Since there is a lot of confusion around the term "marine protected areas," I want to be clear. When I use the term "marine protected area," or "MPA," I mean any area designated to protect the marine environment. When I refer to "no-take" marine reserves, I mean that subset of MPAs that are closed to all extractive activities.

The Need for MPAs

Why do we need MPAs? The answer spans ethical, ecological, and economic considerations. The United States needs a national system of MPAs, including no-take reserves and ocean wilderness areas, to bolster and sustain our dwindling fish populations; to restore the health of our ocean ecosystems; to deepen our understanding of the complexity of ocean life and our impacts on that life; and to ensure that our use of economically valuable marine resources is sustainable over the long term.

No-take reserves also provide urgently needed natural laboratories or "control areas" in which to study the marine environment and the effects of our activities on species and habitats. Without having a full array of control areas—of sufficient size to have meaningful significance on an ecological scale—how will we know whether changes in marine fish and wildlife populations are caused by our management practices or other phenomena, such as global climate change, El Niño, or dust from Africa?

In Florida, we have what we consider to be some of the

most significant and precedent-setting MPAs yet established in the country. The Florida Keys National Marine Sanctuary, at over 2,800 square nautical miles, was significantly larger than any other sanctuary in the country when designated in 1990. The management plan, released in 1995, established different types of zones, focusing higher levels of protection on some of the coral reef habitats thought to be most vulnerable to damage from human activities. This is still the most extensive use of MPA zoning in the U.S., and we hope that this approach will be further refined and applied in other places. As you know, the Tortugas Ecological Reserve and the contiguous Research Natural Area within Dry Tortugas National Park—which we consider together to form the nation's first fully protected ocean wilderness area—was approved [in 2000]. Those of us who were involved in the effort know that establishing such protected areas can be an arduous and complex process. But we also share the feeling that ensuring the protection of the most outstanding coral reef ecosystems in the Tortugas is among the most valuable work we've ever done.

What the Science Tells Us

Study after study, carried out in the U.S. and around the world, tells us that MPAs work. Don't get me wrong: they are not the answer to all of the challenges facing marine conservation and resource management today. They are not a panacea. But if properly designed and managed, they represent the single most comprehensive, robust, and effective ocean management tool available.

Studies also demonstrate that the greatest benefits result from fully protected "no-take" reserves. Protecting an area from fishing leads to rapid increases in biomass, abundance and size of exploited species, and increased biodiversity.

Here are some specifics. In a study of 100 'no-take' areas around the world, researchers discovered that, within the reserves:

- Population density of fish is on average 91 percent higher than outside reserves;
- Biomass—or total living matter in the areas—is 192 percent higher;

- Average size of fish and other organisms is 31 percent higher; and
- Species diversity is 21 percent higher.

Evidence is also mounting that no-take reserves also benefit fisheries in adjacent areas. Some examples: when a reserve in the Philippines was re-opened to fishing, catches collapsed in nearby areas, but then rose again when the reserve was restored. A network of five small reserves in St. Lucia, in the Caribbean, led to increases in catches in adjacent areas of 46 to 90 percent in just five years, despite a 35 percent decrease in the area available for fishing.

One of the best examples of the benefits of MPAs is from Florida. Merritt Island National Wildlife Refuge is due east of here on the other side of the state. This area has been closed to human activities for almost 40 years due to national security concerns at the Kennedy Space Center. Inside the reserve, populations of snook, drum, trout, and mullet are five to 12 times higher than in adjacent areas. Outside the Reserve, recreational fishermen have benefited; this region has consistently produced more world-record-sized black drum, red drum, and spotted sea trout than the rest of Florida waters combined.

We know that in Florida, and throughout our nation's coastal waters, there used to be more and bigger fish. From looking at old scuba magazines, or listening to "old salts"—people who have fished for decades—we know that groupers the size of small cars were common. The Florida Keys was named the "Conch Republic," but has been closed to conch fishing for years because of overfishing. I believe we have not only the chance, but the obligation, to restore the former natural abundance of our seas. I also believe we will never accomplish this unless we move forward decisively with MPAs, no-take reserves, and ocean wilderness.

A Lack of U.S. Leadership

I take pride in the fact that Americans created Yellowstone, the world's first National Park, in 1872. I am less than proud that it took us 100 years to establish the first national marine sanctuary, and that we lag behind Australia, New Zealand, South Africa, and Indonesia in this regard. I think the United

States should be in the vanguard of ocean management. I find it surprising—and disappointing—that so much of the debate about MPAs, and especially about no-take reserves, still seems to be focused on whether or not we need them, rather than how we should best use them to restore the health of our oceans, revitalize our marine industries, and ensure long-term ecological and economic sustainability.

Sharpnack. © 1994 by Joe Sharpnack. Reprinted with permission.

In creating marine protected areas, we are lagging behind other nations, despite calls to act as early as 1966. In its report to President Lyndon Johnson, the Panel on Oceanography of the President's Science Advisory Committee recommended doing what we are still discussing doing 36 years later: establishing a national system of marine wilderness areas. The report, entitled *Effective Use of the Sea*, specifically advised the federal government to "establish a system of marine wilderness preserves." It stated that such a system would represent "an extension of the basic principle established in the Wilderness Act of 1964." And it went further, stating "that it is the policy of the Congress to secure for the American people of present and future generations the benefits of an enduring resource of Wilderness." More recently, the Scientific Consensus Statement on Marine Reserves and Marine Protected Areas, signed by 161 leading marine scientists [in 2000], concluded: "Networks of reserves will be necessary for long-term fishery and conservation benefits." Notice that it says "necessary," not "optional."

How Do We Forge Ahead?

The Ocean Conservancy recommends that this Commission, in its report to the President and Congress, make a firm—and consistent—commitment to the use of MPAs as a marine management tool. For significant progress to occur, a decision must be made and communicated that an adequate national system of MPAs, including no-take reserves and ocean wilderness areas, is essential to protecting the public interest and will be developed. For example, the MPA Executive Order called for "strengthening and expanding" the national MPA system, but provided no new authorities. Second, although the primary purpose of the National Marine Sanctuary Act is "to maintain the natural biological communities in the National Marine Sanctuaries, and to protect, and where appropriate, restore and enhance natural habitats, populations, and ecological processes," most Sanctuaries do little or nothing to restrict fishing. Deadlines for measurable progress toward making sanctuaries a true refuge for fish and other marine species should be set, and progress reviewed regularly.

Although there is no single perfect process for creating MPAs, there are numerous studies documenting approaches to identifying and designating marine protected areas. Based on experiences from around the world, including Florida and California, we recommend that the process of establishing a national system of MPAs incorporate the following guidelines:

    1. ALL stakeholders, not just fishing interests and conservation groups, must be involved in the process from the earliest stages. This is harder than it sounds, and requires deliberate and targeted education and outreach. But we have learned that it is counterproductive to come to the table with maps and boundaries drawn be-

fore the various stakeholders are engaged. The entire process must be collaborative and involve all stakeholders to facilitate discussion and consensus building on what steps are necessary and why.

2. Education is a key first step, and should include a primer on MPAs, describing the different types and objectives of MPAs, "lessons learned" from other places, and a review of the current status of the potential new MPA site, including available biological and socioeconomic information.

3. Discussion should begin by exploring specific objectives. Are there particular species or habitats that warrant special attention? Can specific management targets be set, such as increasing the size or abundance of fish? How "natural" or untouched do we want different areas to be? Are particular activities to be facilitated or restricted?

4. Scientific information is critical and should be referenced at every step of the process: from formulating specific objectives, to setting targets and evaluating alternatives, to measuring success.

The Philosophy Behind MPAs

Beyond the economic and ecological considerations lie ethical ones. To whom do the territorial waters of the United States belong? Like our public lands, our ocean territory is a public resource—it belongs not only to the government, or fishermen, or scientists, or to recreational boaters—but to all of us. Ocean ecosystems and wildlife, including fish, are public resources belonging to all Americans; in that respect they are no different from ecosystems and wildlife on terrestrial public lands. Unlike our lands, all of America's oceans are publicly owned.

On land, we seek to balance resource utilization with conservation of species, habitats, and ecosystems. We have protected nearly 30 percent of our most spectacular lands by establishing national monuments and systems of national parks, national forests, and national wildlife refuges. Approximately 16 percent of those public lands are designated as wilderness areas. In contrast, our ocean policy has given relatively little consideration to the intrinsic value of marine

117

ecosystems and wildlife, or even the finite capacity of our seas to provide food and absorb our wastes. We are now experiencing the ecological and economic consequences of that narrow and short-term vision.

The 1966 report from the President's Science Advisory Committee, to which I referred earlier, speaks to yet another constituency we cannot ignore: future generations. The report indicates that future generations have a right to enjoy "the benefits of an enduring resource of Wilderness."

Clearly, we still have a lot to learn about how marine ecosystems function: how marine species interact with their environments and how habitats in turn relate to their full assemblage of species. I'm confident that future generations will know more about the functioning of healthy marine ecosystems—and their impact on the quality of human life—if we leave them something to work with. In protecting examples of the many different types of ecosystems, biological communities, and habitats found in U.S. waters as the core of a national system of MPAs, Americans may continue to reap endless benefits in the area of science, fisheries, recreation, heritage, and ocean health.

"Plans or suggestions regarding closure of large areas of the U.S. mainland continental shelf to harvest are simply not scientifically supportable from a fishery management perspective."

Fully Protected Marine Reserves Do Not Always Promote Sustainable Fishing

Robert L. Shipp

In the following viewpoint Robert L. Shipp argues that for many fish species traditional methods of conservation such as size limits and quotas more effectively restore overfished stocks than "no-take" marine reserves that close ocean areas to fishing. Advocates of no-take reserves, a type of Marine Protected Area, claim that protected species will spill over into adjacent areas where they can be fished; however, sedentary fish, which in many cases are most in need of protection, do not spill over, Shipp claims. Therefore, he asserts, no-take reserves do little to promote sustainable fishing. Shipp, chair of the Department of Marine Sciences at the University of South Alabama, was chairman of the Gulf of Mexico Fishery Management Council.

As you read, consider the following questions:
1. According to Shipp, what is a fishery management tool?
2. How does creating a "no-take" marine protected area for the benefit of a few fish species affect other species and fishing in adjacent areas, in Shipp's view?

Robert L. Shipp, "'No Take' Marine Protected Areas (nMPAs) as a Fishery Management Tool, a Pragmatic Perspective: A Report to the FishAmerica Foundation," May 23, 2002. Copyright © 2002 by Robert L. Shipp. Reproduced by permission.

A great deal of interest has been expressed in the establishment of Marine Protected Areas (MPAs), marine
"no take" areas, or marine sanctuaries. This interest has
been spurred by the frequent references to depleted fish
stocks, and continued decline in marine fishery resources.

Proponents of so called "no take" Marine Protected Areas
(nMPAs) have described the benefits to include potential as
a fishery management tool as well as several other related
advantages, specifically, conserving biodiversity, protecting
(coastal) ecosystem integrity, preserving cultural heritage,
providing educational and recreational opportunities, and
establishing sites for scientific research. In addition, other
benefits suggested include enhancing ecotourism, and reducing user group conflict (e.g. divers and harvesters).

The concept of nMPAs is initially attractive, and will no
doubt elicit a great deal of support and discussion among
various groups interested in protecting marine habitats.
However, the many offered benefits described above often
overlap, and become intertwined in the discussions that en-
sue. *A fishery management tool is one that sustains and/or increases through time the yield of a fish stock, or several sympatric
stocks of an ecosystem.* If nMPAs are to be considered as a management tool, then that goal or objective, sustained and/or
increased yield, needs to be clearly stated, and distinguished
from other, more theoretical goals.

Using Traditional Management Tools

Traditional management tools generally focus on reducing
effort, enhancing stocks from hatchery operations, and protecting critical habitat. Effort reduction includes bag and size
limits (including sometimes slot limits), quotas, seasonal
and/or areal closures, gear restrictions, and by-catch reduction. These have been successful for more than a century in
freshwater environments. Their use in marine habitats has
only become widespread in the United States in recent
decades, especially since passage of the Fishery Conservation
and Management Act in 1976. Hatchery operations and
stocking have also been primarily a freshwater endeavor, although recent efforts to stock some marine species have been
attempted and yet to be evaluated over the long term. Pro-

tection of critical marine habitats has become an issue of extreme concern and is the focus of current efforts on the part of all Fishery Management Councils, as required in the most recent reauthorization of the Sustainable Fisheries Act. . . .

NMPAs may serve many purposes, . . . but when intended to serve as a fishery management tool, there are several situations for which they may be extremely beneficial, and many others for which more traditional methods are much preferred. These are reviewed briefly as follows.

The Benefits of "No-Take" Reserves

NMPAs can have a strong beneficial impact for fishery management during periods of active spawning by aggregations, when species may be especially vulnerable to harvest, and when certain components of the stock (e.g. large male gag grouper) may be disproportionately liable to capture. This can lead to imbalanced sex ratios that can further jeopardize a stressed stock. The utility of these is likely to be seasonal, and normally would not require year around catch restrictions.

In instances where a stock is severely overfished and subject to little or no management, an nMPA can be used along with other measures to more rapidly replenish populations. This is especially true in isolated, insular populations that are not strongly connected to proximal populations for replenishment.

Where habitats are damaged by fishing practices, establishment of nMPAs may help ensure habitat recovery. This is useful when these habitats, such as submerged aquatic vegetation, reef structures or other hard bottom habitat, are critical for vulnerable life stages. Oftentimes, however, gear restrictions can be enacted to lessen the social impact that would result in declaration of a total no-take zone.

NMPAs may also be beneficial where ecosystem management is employed in fisheries (primarily of near sedentary species) where by-catch of non-targeted species has become excessive, or conversely, where a protected species has reached population levels which increase natural mortality rates of targeted species, preventing a reasonable harvest. An nMPA will allow some version of dynamic equilibrium to return. When the equilibrium has been reestablished, then alternate, more traditional management actions may be desirable to allow yield from the system, However, ecosystem based management is still in its infancy, and much research needs to be done before tested management principles can be established.

The Liabilities of "No-Take" Reserves

When establishment of an nMPA is intended as a near proxy for a virgin stock, several factors need to be kept in mind. And it might be helpful, in gaining perspective, to recall that some of these principles have been well known for decades or longer, though sometimes forgotten. First, by definition, a virgin stock provides no yield. Therefore a perfect proxy would be a negative in terms of management goals to produce an MSY [maximum sustainable yield] or OY [optimum yield]. However, proponents of nMPA usage for management purposes refer to a "spillover effect" of harvestable adults to adjacent areas. The impact of this spillover will always be less than that of a properly managed stock, which generates the optimal yield-per-recruit, again, by definition. These models are discussed in numerous classical and modern texts.

A Permanent Loss of Fishery Productivity

The widespread establishment of no-take reserves poses more of a threat to the productivity of marine fisheries than does overfishing. I say that because I believe that we are on our way to improving fishery productivity by reducing fishing effort. This ability to reverse overfishing and rebuild fishery productivity contrasts with the permanent loss of fishery productivity that will be caused by no-take reserves.

Richard B. Allen, "No-Take Reserves as a Fishery Management Tool," speech delivered at Fisheries, Oceanography, and Society: A Symposium Presented by the Ocean Life Institute, August 27, 2001.

The issue of spillover is addressed briefly by [Ed] Houde [and the Committee on the Evaluation, Design, and Monitoring of Marine Reserves and Protected Areas in the United States] (2001). The authors describe the difficulty of direct confirmation of spillover effects, and suggest models may be more useful in understanding how marine reserves function in a regional context. But they also note that those conclusions are limited by underlying assumptions on which the model is based. For species with low mobility, the spillover is minimal, yet these sedentary species are the very ones for which an nMPA is supposedly most effective.

Another claim is that larvae from an nMPA will be a significant addition to the overall stocks. This may be beneficial, but only for a very seriously depleted stock. In other cases, larval production, always in excess of the carrying capacity of the habitat, does not normally relate to year class strength. Rather density dependent factors usually control ultimate recruitment to the harvestable stock. While this principle has been the subject of scores of books and probably thousands of publications, it was espoused nearly 150 years ago by Darwin and restated frequently in most every fishery text.

And much more recently, data presented by the GOMFMC [Gulf of Mexico Fishery Management Council] Coastal Pelagic Stock Assessment Panel (January 2002) reemphasizes for very practical management purposes, such as in the case of Gulf king mackerel, that egg production does not correlate to an increase in stock size, the panel stating: "recruitment is assumed to increase to some level of spawning stock, and then to remain at the average recruitment for higher spawning stock values."

The Stocks Within an nMPA

There are numerous examples in the literature of stock increases within an nMPA. However, one must not forget what the point is here in regard to yield. While effective nMPAs may support a stock with relatively greater biomass, perhaps larger individuals, and a higher spawning potential ratio (SPR), this portion of the stock has been removed from harvest. Therefore, the overall yield is reduced by whatever fraction could be contributed to overall harvest from this protected stock, and mitigated only by the possibility of spillover or larval contribution, as discussed above.

A Pragmatic Perspective

Examination of the scores of coastal species from the mid to south Atlantic, Gulf, and U.S. Pacific coasts reveals that very few species are known to be both overfished and/or experiencing overfishing, and are sedentary. Those candidates that are in both categories, and may possibly benefit from an nMPA are found in widely differing geographic ranges, with optimal potential nMPA sites far apart (e.g. lingcod and surf perch in the Pacific, red porgy in the Atlantic and gray triggerfish in the Gulf). To establish an nMPA for the benefit of those few species would remove harvest potential of the scores of sympatric forms, most of which are not overfished. And while this may not reduce the overall harvest of these species, it would definitely reduce efficiency and increase fishing effort in other, adjacent areas.

Far better would be to impose more traditional methods to restore the overfished stocks, as has been done for many species. This becomes more and more successful as we adopt more precautionary harvest levels, improve our methods of stock assessment, stock/recruit relationships, and life history information. . . .

Plans or suggestions regarding closure of large areas of the U.S. mainland continental shelf to harvest are simply not scientifically supportable from a fishery management perspective. The suggestion, for example, that as much as 40% of the Southern California shelf should be designated an nMPA is totally without merit from a fishery harvest perspective. Though there may be other aesthetic benefits, such a closure would severely reduce harvest potentials, shift effort to other areas, and likely have a substantial negative economic impact on both the commercial and recreational fishing industries.

"*[Individual Fishing Quotas] are a far superior approach to traditional regulations in correcting the problems of overfishing and overcapacity.*"

Individual Fishing Quotas Will Benefit U.S. Fisheries

Donald R. Leal

Individual Fishing Quotas (IFQs), the permission to catch a percentage of the scientifically determined total allowable catch (TAC) in a fishery, are the best solution to the problem of overfishing, argues Donald R. Leal in the following viewpoint, originally given as testimony before the House Subcommittee on Fisheries Conservation, Wildlife, and Oceans. IFQs safeguard each fisher's allocation of fish each year, thus discouraging the "race for the fish," which promotes wasteful and often dangerous fishing strategies. Establishing fair methods for allocating how much fish each fisher can catch each year will help make IFQs an accepted strategy to promote sustainable fishing. Leal is a senior associate at the Political Economy Research Center in Bozeman, Montana.

As you read, consider the following questions:
1. What does Leal say are the advantages of the fact that IFQs are transferable?
2. In the author's opinion, what is one obvious way to address potential unfairness in the allocation of quotas?
3. According to Leal, what is the secondary impact of taxing away quota value?

Donald R. Leal, testimony before the Subcommittee on Fisheries Conservation, Wildlife, and Oceans, Committee on Resources, U.S. House of Representatives, Washington, DC, February 13, 2002.

M r. Chairman and members of the Subcommittee, thank you for the opportunity to testify on individual fishing quotas (IFQs) as they relate to reauthorization of the Magnuson-Stevens Act. Because IFQs affect both wealth and the structural makeup in a fishery, the subcommittee expressed interest in hearing views on a number of issues related to the use of IFQs. Before launching into these issues, I would like to point out something at the outset: IFQs arose in response to significant problems plaguing many U.S. fisheries—namely, overharvesting, overcapitalization, falling fisher income, poor product quality, and hazardous fishing.

These are problems that decades of traditional regulations—restrictions on fishing vessels and gear, area fished, fishing times, and a total allowable catch (TAC)—have failed to solve. Indeed in a number of cases they have exacerbated these problems. For example, in the Alaska halibut fishery prior to IFQs, season duration was progressively shortened to prevent actual harvest from exceeding the total allowable catch (TAC). Not only did actual harvests often exceed the TAC, fishermen overinvested in vessels, gear and labor in an attempt to win the race for fish. The compressed fishing season also forced fishermen to fish under hectic and sometimes dangerous conditions. There was enormous waste of halibut from lost or abandoned gear and from spoilage. Fresh fish was delivered over short periods which led to market gluts and frozen halibut for consumers for most of the year.

The Success of IFQs

IFQs have eliminated or significantly reduced these problems. By allowing managers to extend the fishing season from a few days to about 8 months, fresh halibut is available for most of the year; fishing safety is vastly improved; the amount of fish lost to abandoned gear has fallen dramatically, and annual harvest goals are being met.

Fleet excesses have also been reduced as intended. Some vessel owners and crew have exited the fishery but new entrants, including hired skippers and crews under the old regime, are now quota holders in the fishery. According to Alaska's Commercial Fisheries Entry Commission, previous crew members acquired after four years of the program anywhere from 9 to 17 percent of the quota share units outstanding depending on the region fished.

The Alaska halibut fishery exemplifies the kinds of improvements that have occurred in other fisheries under IFQs around the world. Overall, IFQs have reduced overcapitalization in the fishery, raised fisher income, reduced hazardous fishing, improved product quality, and importantly, when IFQs represent permanent shares, as they do in New Zealand, they have encouraged fishermen to cooperate and invest in improving the health of fish stocks.

A Superior Management Tool

On the question of whether IFQs be used as a management tool, the evidence is clear. IFQs are a far superior approach to traditional regulations in correcting the problems of overfishing and overcapacity. As such, I recommend that Congress lift the moratorium on the development and implementation of IFQ programs.

IFQs work because they give the holder the certainty that his or her allocation of the TAC will not be taken by someone else. This certainty has proven very effective at mitigating the race for the fish. Moreover, because they are transferable, IFQs can be very effective in reducing overcapitalization plaguing so many U.S. fisheries. Rather than engaging in a losing proposition, less efficient fishers sell their quota shares and move on while more efficient fishers work to reduce fishing costs and produce more value in the fishery.

Increasing IFQ Acceptance

The one drawback as IFQs are defined under current U.S. law is that the incentive for fishers to act collectively in husbanding the resource and in complying with regulations for conservation is hampered by the lack of permanency of quota shares. To enhance fishermen cooperation to conserve the resource an IFQ should be made a permanent right to a percentage share of the TAC.

There has been much controversy on the initial allocation of IFQs. Typically IFQs are allocated to individual vessel owners on the basis of their catch history in a fishery. The rationale for selecting vessel owners and using their catch history is that it provides a quantitative way of taking into account prior investment in developing the fishery. As evidence by the near universal use of this approach in IFQ fisheries around the world, it appears to be the most acceptable approach for initial allocation, at least among current participants.

Putting an End to Wasteful Practices

With IFQs I see a fishery that can once again be enjoyable, that one can take some pride in. No more need to throw away perfectly good fish. No more missed openers because of sickness or breakdowns. No more attempts to go offshore during a gale. . . .

No more "take-it-or-leave-it" prices from dealers and no more rotting gluts of fish in their storage facilities. In my mind, the advantages far outweigh the concerns!

Felix Cox, *National Fisherman*, December 2000.

This approach is not free of criticisms, however. Long delays between the time period used for determining a participant's catch history and implementation of IFQs can lead to controversy. In the Alaska halibut fishery, for example, a long delay in implementation resulted in the exclusion of some fishers who were active in the fishery just prior to IFQs but not active during the time period used to determine catch history. Understandably, these fishers felt they were making the investments in developing the fishery but being left out of initial allocation of quotas. To avoid such controversy, the time between the control period used in determining catch history for initial allocation and the implementation of IFQs should be as short as possible.

There are other criticisms related to this approach. Since IFQs are allocated free of charge no revenue is generated from this process. Critics charge that giving away quota amounts to a windfall gain for current participants. In addition, individuals like hired skippers and crew with no record of catch history can feel they are being treated unfairly. Also, processors may experience lower returns from their investments because of market changes that IFQs bring about.

One obvious way to address these concerns is through the

use of auctions for initial allocation. Such an approach is not unprecedented for a public resource—e.g., spectra rights. An auction will generate revenue upfront and allocate quota shares efficiently, if shares are to go to the highest bidder. But an auction can also be modified so individuals who have invested in developing the fishery have at least a price preference in their bids over other bidders. Such an approach can be effective in retaining a majority of prior investors while generating revenue for the government. However, given the fact that bidders will vary in their ability to access financial capital, auctions will probably not eliminate the perception of an "unfairness" in initial allocation. As such, awarding initial allocations on the basis of catch history still appears to be the most attractive option at this time with some modifications.

One modification is that councils should allocate a percentage of the TAC to local fishing communities likely to suffer some employment reductions in transitioning to IFQs. These communities, in turn, would have the option of either hiring displaced skippers and crews to fish their allocation or sell or lease to them shares of their allocation. While such an approach may require current participants to give up a fraction of their historical allocations, the willingness to do so should be enhanced by the potential for IFQs to change incentives from maximizing catches to maximizing returns.

In the case of processors, there appears to be no compelling argument for mandating initial quota shares to processors across all fisheries adopting IFQs. Evidence indicates processor impacts will differ on a case by case basis. In cases where councils determine that processors will be adversely affected by IFQs, another modification is that councils offer them some form of compensation, such as buyouts of obsolete and unmalleable capital.

Monitoring and Enforcement

The costs of monitoring and enforcement in a fishery increases under IFQs. Unfortunately, information is quite limited on the magnitude of these. Data from British Columbia and Alaska's halibut fisheries gives us some idea of enforcement costs relative to ex vessel price. In 1993, $0.067 per lb., or 3 percent of ex vessel price, was spent on enforcement in the British Columbia halibut IFQ fishery. For the Alaska halibut fishery under IFQs, an estimated $0.073 per lb., or a modest 4 percent of ex vessel price, was spent on enforcement in 1997. In any case, quota holders stand to benefit greatly from IFQs and thus should pay the full costs of managing IFQs.

Some argue for an additional annual tax on quota value. This is based on the belief that as trustee of a public resource the government should receive the associated economic surplus or economic rent, which is capitalized along with other profits in quota value and not easily measured. This argument, however, fails to consider the secondary impacts of taxing away quota value. For one, as [Ronald N.] Johnson (1995) argues in an article in *Marine Resource Economics*, the industry becomes less motivated to conserve the exploited resource preferring that the government set a higher overall harvest level even if it means lower abundance in the future. Moreover, as profit maximizers, private operators are in the best position to lower fishing costs and raise product value in the fishery. The government has neither the willingness nor the ability to do the same. By taxing away quota value the incentive for quota holders to act collectively in lowering costs and improving product value in the fishery is reduced. Indeed taxing away quota value may actually result in lower returns to the treasury than from a fishery whose main source of revenues are taxes from ordinary income. Thus, quota holders should be allowed to retain the full value of their IFQs.

Monitoring and enforcement is part and parcel of management costs and is critical to maintaining the integrity of an IFQ system. To ensure system integrity, councils must require a dual-channel reporting system comprised of fish harvesters and their buyers as well as stiff penalties to discourage cheating. All fish receivers—fish wholesalers and processors—are required to report fish purchased from fishers. All fish permit holders are required to provide detailed catch reports along with information on effort (vessel, area fished, and the quota share fished) after each fishing trip. Penalties must be stiff enough to deter cheating. This would include forfeiture of quota shares for repeated violations.

In sum, experience with IFQs prove they are superior to regulations in ending the race for the fish. They can be controversial, but I hope that the above recommendations can help mitigate some of the concerns so we as a nation can move forward by allowing IFQs as a management tool to rebuild our nation's fisheries.

"[Individual Transferable Quotas] have major socioeconomic impacts on fishers and the fishing fleet, encouraging concentration of fishing rights in fewer hands."

Individual Fishing Quotas May Not Benefit Fisheries

Kaitilin Gaffney

In the following viewpoint Kaitilin Gaffney argues that the benefits of Individual Transferable Quotas (ITQs), the permission to catch a percentage of the total allowable catch of a fishery, may not outweigh the costs. Gaffney claims that small-scale fishers often sell their quotas to bigger companies, thus concentrating fishing rights in the hands of a few. Moreover, the author points out, ITQs do not necessarily prevent the depletion of fish. In New Zealand, Gaffney maintains for example, ITQs did not protect orange roughy from overfishing. Gaffney, who spent 1997 studying New Zealand's ITQ system, is an environmental attorney in Santa Cruz, California.

As you read, consider the following questions:
1. According to Gaffney, what do ITQ advocates argue will happen when fishers are given ownership rights to fish resources?
2. In the author's opinion, what do local communities in southwest Alaska argue happened as a result of the allocation of halibut ITQs?
3. What happened when ITQs were introduced in Iceland, in Gaffney's view?

Kaitilin Gaffney, "Can ITQs End Overfishing?" *Coast and Ocean*, Summer 1998. Copyright © 1998 by California Coast and Ocean. Reproduced by permission of the publisher and the author.

C onventional wisdom attributes the problems facing marine fisheries to the open-access nature of the resource. Because no one owns the fish in the sea, fishers have no incentive to conserve. The result, to use a phrase coined by Garrett Hardin, professor emeritus of the Environmental Studies Department at the University of California, Santa Barbara, is the "tragedy of the commons": users compete to get as much as possible, each for himself, thus inevitably depleting the resource all share in common. Attempts to manage the resource by traditional methods, such as restrictions on fishing gear and limited seasons, may only exacerbate the self-defeating competition. Fishers invest in bigger boats and more sophisticated gear in a race to catch as much as they can while the stocks last, thus accelerating the fishery's decline.

Privatizing Fish Stocks

In the latest attempt to find a way out of this dilemma, some economists recommend that fish stocks be privatized via a system of transferable harvesting quotas. Such Individual Transferable Quota (ITQ) systems in effect create limited property rights to the fish in the sea, since only those who own a quota are allowed to fish. Advocates claim that ITQs ensure biological sustainability while simultaneously promoting economic efficiency.

The basic idea is this: After government fisheries biologists determine a sustainable total catch level for a fish stock, the total is divided into ITQs. Each unit of quota entitles the holder to harvest a predetermined percentage of the total catch. Advocates argue that by giving fishers ownership rights to the resource, ITQ systems end the tragedy of the commons, instead fostering a sense of stewardship and encouraging conservation. Critics, however, point to issues that have emerged as such systems have been put into practice, and argue for caution.

Because ITQs can be bought and sold, market forces determine who participates in the fishery and at what level. It is expected, for example, that fishers with low operating costs will buy ITQs from their less efficient competitors.

Described by some as the "emission trading program of the sea," ITQs are being promoted as a cost-effective management tool. They are gaining popularity, in this era of growing privatization, as an opportunity for government to step back and let the free market manage marine resources.

A Moratorium

Currently, ITQs are not used in any California fishery. In 1995, the Department of Fish and Game considered adopting individual fishing quotas for the southern California sea urchin fishery, but dropped the proposal when it failed to gain industry support. At the federal level, ITQ regimes are currently limited to the Alaskan halibut and sablefish, Atlantic quahog and surfclam, and South Atlantic wreckfish fisheries. During the 1996 reauthorization of the Magnuson Act, which governs federal fisheries management, Congress directed the National Academy of Sciences to study ITQs; it then enacted a four-year moratorium on new ITQ regimes pending the outcome of that study. A committee appointed by the Academy has held hearings around the nation and is currently developing recommendations regarding a national policy on ITQs. Its report, . . . ["Sharing the Fish: Toward a National Policy on Individual Fishing Quotas" was published in 1999].

ITQ advocates have criticized the current U.S. moratorium as a political maneuver by Alaskan legislators concerned that ITQs might benefit the Seattle-based fleet over home-state interests. Local communities in southwest Alaska, however, argue that the allocation of halibut ITQs essentially rewarded highly overcapitalized fishing fleets that had put the resource at risk, while punishing communities that had fished sustainably for hundreds of years.

In fact, small local fishers were pushed out before the system was even in place. When the season was severely restricted, they could no longer compete with overcapitalized boats. It was not worth it for them to go out for two days: they only had small boats; the weather might be bad; it was dangerous. They therefore bowed out in the face of hundreds of big boats. Then, a few years later, ITQs were allocated based on a time period in which they did not participate. Because they had let their halibut fishing lapse, they were left out of the allocation.

The Benefits

Although ITQs are the most recent trend in fisheries management and appear to be the tool of choice for many, much of the critical acclaim the system has received is based on theoretical benefits rather than actual results of ITQ systems. A review of ITQ implementation, both in the United States and abroad, suggests that Congress may be right to approach ITQs with caution.

The benefits of ITQs, though still debated, are potentially significant. By guaranteeing fishers a right to harvest a share of the catch, the quotas provide a level of security that, in turn, promotes rational harvesting that benefits both fishers and consumers. There are positive impacts for both fisher and consumer as well. In Alaska's halibut fishery, the season was limited to two 24-hour periods each year before ITQs were introduced. Hundreds of vessels participated in the frantic "race to fish." Boats were filled dangerously beyond capacity as skippers tried to maximize catch during the short—but incredibly valuable—season. Now under ITQ management, the Alaskan halibut season runs from April 15 to November 15 each year: eight months. Longer seasons provide fresh fish for consumers for a longer period and allow safer harvesting conditions for fishers.

The Disadvantages

There is a downside to the system as well, however. ITQs have major socioeconomic impacts on fishers and the fishing fleet, encouraging concentration of fishing rights in fewer hands; they may be prohibitively expensive to administer; and they may fail to resolve—and, indeed, may aggravate—the waste of resources known as the bycatch problem.

The initial challenge of ITQ management is allocation. Who should receive ITQs? Quotas are usually distributed on the basis of historical catch during a defined eligibility period, with the amount alloted to individual fishers designed to reflect the level of participation in the fishery during the designated period. Claims of unfairness and inequity may be inevitable. They may also be accurate. When New Zealand adopted ITQs, part-time commercial fishers were excluded from the allocation, and more than 2,000 people whose livelihood depended on fishing were left out of the system.

ITQs can cause changes in the structure of the fishing fleet as individual owner-operators sell their ITQs to larger-scale fishing companies and quotas are consolidated into fewer and fewer hands. When ITQs were introduced in Iceland, many fishers sold their quota and then leased it back, fishing for a percentage of the catch. Crew members who had traditionally been paid a fixed share of the catch had to accept only a share of the captain's share. Decreases in crew wages led to social unrest that culminated in national strikes in 1994 and 1995. In 11 years under ITQs, New Zealand's three largest fishing companies increased their combined percentage of total ITQ holdings from 25 to 55 percent, and ten companies now own more than 80 percent of all ITQs. Similar issues of ITQ concentration and changed industry structure are reported from Nova Scotia. As for the issue of cost-effectiveness, it is possible that ITQ systems may turn out to be prohibitively expensive to administer and enforce effectively. They require regulatory agencies to monitor each fisher's catch to ensure it does not exceed the allotment. And because fishers want to fill their quotas with the highest-grade fish possible, ITQs constitute an incentive for smaller or less valuable fish to be discarded.

Depending upon Good Science

ITQ systems share limitations with other management models. They depend on accurate and timely scientific research—which is sometimes impossible to come by. To set total catch at an appropriate level, scientists must know the population size and biologic characteristics of each species and must understand environmental factors that affect the species. This is no easy task. As one frustrated fisheries biologist noted, it's hard to get an accurate head count under water, for fish generally don't raise their fins when you call attendance.

Other management regimes use the total allowable catch concept too, but usually it's applied more loosely, for instance by correlating the season length with the amount of fish that managers think is sustainable. If fisher's increase their capacity, they might exceed the target total; if conditions are poor or the stocks aren't doing so well, the fish are harder to catch and total catch may be less. With ITQs the season is longer—maybe even lasting all year—so the total will likely be caught even if the stocks are dropping and harder to catch. Therefore, ITQs appear to be more dependent on good science, though all management regimes are clearly vulnerable to poor information.

New Zealand learned the importance of fisheries research the hard way in the late 1980s, when its most valuable fishery collapsed after catch levels were set too high. First discovered in the 1970s, orange roughy was subject to intensive exploitation in spite of the fact that scientists lacked even the most basic understanding of the species. New Zealand's orange roughy fishery was managed by ITQ. . . . Although the necessity of rigorous research is not unique to ITQ systems, the orange roughy example serves as an important reminder that ITQs have inherent limitations.

A Need for Caution

ITQs are not a panacea. Although they may prove a useful tool for fisheries managers, the jury is still out on whether the benefits they provide outweigh their costs. Caution in adopting ITQ regimes is further warranted because once they are adopted they may be practically irreversible: the fact that they ostensibly create a form of individual property rights means there would be enormous political resistance to any attempt to abolish them.

The challenges facing fisheries, both in California and around the world, do not have easy answers. It is to be hoped that a legacy of the International Year of the Ocean [1998] will be an increased commitment to exploring a wide range of potential solutions to the management challenges presented by the sea and the coast.

"The federal framework to protect the environment from potential impacts of offshore aquaculture might be termed an unfinished patchwork, with holes and mismatches."

Federal Regulation of Aquaculture Is Necessary

Rebecca J. Goldburg

Fish farming, known as aquaculture, is a growing U.S. industry. Rebecca J. Goldburg maintains in the following viewpoint that federal agencies must design new regulations to protect the marine environment from aquaculture's impact. For example, the Environmental Protection Agency should set strict guidelines to control aquaculture effluent from polluting nearby waters, she argues. In addition, controls should be established to protect wild fish, which are being depleted for use as feed for farmed fish. According to Goldburg, wild fish are also endangered when they breed with genetically engineered farmed fish that escape their pens, which can weaken wild fish's ability to survive. Goldburg is a senior scientist at the Environmental Defense Fund.

As you read, consider the following questions:
1. In Goldburg's opinion, what is the most environmentally controversial type of aquaculture in the United States?
2. In what ways might transgenic fish harm wild fish populations, in the author's view?
3. According to Goldburg, what is one of the main impediments to the restoration of wild Atlantic salmon?

Rebecca J. Goldburg, testimony before the U.S. Commission on Ocean Policy, July 23, 2002.

Aquaculture is seen by many experts as the best means to boost the global seafood supply. The total global fisheries catch has peaked, and significantly greater quantities of wild fish are unlikely to be obtained from the seas. Aquaculture is the only available means to significantly supplement fisheries catches at a time when world population and affluence are increasing.

Aquaculture production worldwide has grown rapidly in recent decades, and at a somewhat slower rate in the United States. Freshwater catfish dominate US aquaculture production, which totals almost $1 billion per year. Marine fish, chiefly oysters, clams, and salmon, are roughly a third of US aquaculture production by weight. Growth in production varies considerably by species, with production of farmed Atlantic salmon and hard clam enjoying considerable growth in recent years.

Like other forms of animal production, aquaculture can cause environmental degradation, although the extent and type of environmental impacts varies considerably with the type of fish raised and the production system used. The most environmentally controversial type of aquaculture in the United States is salmon farming in coastal netpens. Not only are salmon farms placed directly in public waters, but the porous nature of netpens means that salmon wastes are discharged directly into coastal waters, and as I discuss below, that cultivated salmon frequently escape farms. In contrast, cultivation of filter-feeding mollusks, which clean water by removing particles, is far less controversial.

In my testimony . . . I would like to highlight five issues and recommendations related to federal oversight of and programs for aquaculture, including one issue that is especially pressing here in New England.

Developing Aquaculture Effluent Guidelines

Wastewater discharges from fish farms can contain large amounts of fish feces and uneaten feed. For example, by one estimate a salmon farm of 200,000 fish releases an amount of nitrogen, phosphorous, and fecal matter roughly equivalent to the nutrient waste in untreated sewage from 20,000, 25,000, and 60,000 people respectively. In addition, discharges can include chemicals such as antibiotics and "biological pollutants" such as bacteria, parasites and escaped fish.

Under the Clean Water Act, the Environmental Protection Agency (EPA) must develop industry-by-industry "effluent guidelines"—essentially national minimum standards for wastewater discharge permits. EPA has never developed effluent guidelines for aquaculture, although under the terms of a consent decree the agency must now promulgate guidelines for aquaculture by June 2004. It is critical that these guidelines address the range of potential environmental impacts from aquaculture discharges by encompassing biological pollutants as well as the nutrients and other chemical pollutants more traditionally considered by EPA.

Recommendation: EPA should promulgate effluent guidelines for aquaculture. Depending on the aquaculture system, these guidelines should include limits on nutrients, total suspended solids, human and non-human pathogens, pesticides, antibiotics, and biological impairments due to the introduction of non-native organisms. Along with regulating effluents, federal agencies could provide incentives, such as loans and cost-share programs, for aquaculturists to adopt pollution prevention measures.

Regulating Offshore Aquaculture

The National Oceanic and Atmospheric Administration (NOAA) is promoting offshore aquaculture—aquaculture in the exclusive economic zone (EEZ) [an area extending 200 miles from the U.S. coastline, over which the federal government has control]—as a means to expand aquaculture in areas where there are fewer user conflicts than closer to shore. However, to be commercially profitable, offshore aquaculture facilities will need to offset the substantial costs of establishing and maintaining offshore facilities by raising valuable fish on a large scale. Huge offshore finfish farms might well suffer similar environmental problems to those that now dog nearshore salmon farms.

The federal framework to protect the environment from potential impacts of offshore aquaculture might be termed an unfinished patchwork, with holes and mismatches. The resulting uncertainties has meant an ad hoc and often unsatisfactory application of federal laws to the few offshore aquaculture projects that have proceeded to the point where developers sought approvals. The Army Corps of Engineers (ACOE) has taken the lead in regulating offshore facilities, issuing permits under the Rivers and Harbors Act of 1899 and the Outer Continental Shelf Lands Act. The ACOE does not, however, have a clear legal mandate under either of these statutes to protect the environment and lacks expertise to weigh the full ecological impacts of offshore aquaculture facilities.

Recommendation: Through a combination of regulatory and legislative changes, offshore aquaculture facilities should be required to receive both discharge permits from EPA under the Clean Water Act and an approval from the National Marine Fisheries Service (NMFS) based on a standard of "no significant adverse effect on marine resources."

If a new agency for oceans governance was created, as is sometimes proposed in oceans policy circles, it could assume lead responsibility for oversight of offshore aquaculture.

Monitoring Genetically Engineered Fish

A number of researchers have now created transgenic fish—fish that have been altered via genetic engineering techniques to have added genetic material. Fish are genetically engineered with the intention of introducing or amplifying an economically valuable trait, and one US company is now trying to commercialize salmon genetically engineered for faster growth. The escape of these or other transgenic fish from fish farms could harm wild fish populations through interbreeding, if introduced genes spread through wild fish populations and ultimately weakened them. Escaped transgenic fish could also harm wild fish through increased competition or predation.

The Food and Drug Administration (FDA) has decided to regulate transgenic fish and other animals as animal drugs. However, while FDA is the appropriate agency to regulate the safety of these fish as food, it lacks an environmental mandate and expertise necessary to protect against the potential ecological effects of transgenic fish. Moreover, under drug law FDA must keep all information about a pending drug application, including even its existence, confidential.

The only exception is for information publicly disclosed by the manufacturer. Thus the public cannot generally participate in FDA decision-making about transgenic fish, for example by providing comments.

Recommendation: Congress should amend federal law so that the approval of transgenic fish for commercial sale requires evidence of ecological as well as food safety, and the approval process is transparent and open to public participation.

Reducing Aquaculture's Dependence on Wild Fisheries

With the exception of salmon farming, US aquaculture is dominated by small and mid-sized companies with a limited capacity to support research and development activities. Government funded research thus plays a large role in the development of new technologies and management practices for US aquaculture.

How Much Wild Fish Is Needed to Produce 1 Kg of Farmed Salmon?

1 kg of fish feed for salmon or trout consists on average of 280g of fish oil. To produce 1 kg of fish oil, around 12 kg of wild caught fish is needed, depending on species and season. The average feed factor in Norway is 1.2 kg. To produce 1 kg of salmon:

$$280g \times 1.2 = 330.6g \text{ of fish oil}$$
$$330.6g \times 12 = 3967g \text{ of wild caught fish}$$

1kg of salmon requires 4kg of wild caught fish

Taija-Riita Tuominen and Maren Esmark, *Food for Thought: The Use of Marine Resources in Fish Feed*, WWF Norway, February 2003.

Targeted research could help to reduce a number of aquaculture's environmental impacts. A prime example is the use of fishmeal and fish oil as key components of feed for many farmed finfish and crustaceans. Since most fishmeal and fish oil are made from wild caught fish, farming some types of fish can require several times the amount of wild fish as inputs as is ultimately obtained in farmed fish outputs. These aquaculture systems actually deplete rather than supplement wild fisheries, and there are strong ecological and economic rationales for lessening aquaculture's dependence on wild fish for feed.

Recommendation: Appropriations to NOAA and other federal agencies for aquaculture research should target key environmental goals. One goal should be to reduce aquaculture's dependence on fisheries inputs by reducing the fishmeal and fish oil content of feed and by emphasizing the farming of fish that feed at low trophic levels (i.e. that are not highly carnivorous).

Protecting Endangered Wild Salmon

Wild salmon runs are listed as endangered on both the east and west coasts of the United States, including the remaining runs of Atlantic salmon in Maine. The escape of Atlantic salmon from Maine salmon farms has been identified by NMFS and the US Fish and Wildlife Service (USFWS) as one of the major impediments to restoration of wild Atlantic salmon, largely because of the potential genetic harm to the few remaining wild salmon from interbreeding between escaped farmed and wild fish. The result has been conflict between salmon farming and conservation interests, since Atlantic salmon is the primary species of salmon farmed and Maine is the largest center of salmon farming in the United States.

NMFS and USFWS have proposed a number of reasonable measures, such as better containment of farmed salmon and disease control measures for farmed salmon, in order to minimize the impact of salmon farms on endangered wild salmon. However, such technologies and practices have not yet been broadly adopted by salmon farmers, and salmon farming continues to jeopardize wild Atlantic salmon.

Recommendation: Federal officials should support NMFS and USFWS decisions and activities to protect remaining wild salmon runs, including measures that require alteration of salmon farming practices.

Aquaculture is the only means to significantly add to seafood supplies, and the industry should and will undoubtedly continue to grow. The challenge is for aquaculture to grow in a manner that truly augments fisheries and does not harm marine ecosystems. There are a number of steps that the federal government can take to answer this challenge.

> *"Legal and regulatory obstacles are commonly cited as major impediments to U.S. aquaculture growth and development."*

Alternatives to Government Regulation Will Promote the Growth of Aquaculture

Ferdinand F. Wirth and E. Jane Luzar

In the following viewpoint Ferdinand F. Wirth and E. Jane Luzar argue that fish farming, known as aquaculture, must increase to meet the global demand for seafood. However, aquaculture uses natural, public resources and is thus subject to numerous state and federal agencies whose rigid regulations encumber rather than encourage the industry, the authors maintain. In contrast, free-market incentives—such as charging businesses for emissions—can encourage competition and environmental stewardship, they claim. Wirth is professor of food and resource economics and Luzar is associate dean of the College of Agricultural and Life Sciences at the University of Florida.

As you read, consider the following questions:
1. According to Wirth and Luzar, how much will aquaculture production have to grow to meet worldwide seafood demand?
2. In the opinion of A. Markandya and J. Richardson, what does the cost-minimizing firm do when faced with emission charges or credits?

Ferdinand F. Wirth and E. Jane Luzar, "Environmental Management of the U.S. Aquaculture Industry: Insights from a National Survey," *Society and Natural Resources*, vol. 12, October/November 1999, pp. 659–72. Copyright © 1999 by Taylor & Francis, www.routledge-ny.com. Reproduced by permission.

A quaculture, an aquatic form of agriculture, is the rearing of aquatic plants and animals under controlled or semi-controlled conditions. Aquaculture has been practiced for over 2000 years in Asia and is the fastest growing food-producing industry in the world today. Increasing worldwide demand for fish and shellfish, diminishing supplies and increasing costs of wild-caught fish and shellfish, and greater consistency in supply and quality of cultured fish and shellfish have contributed to the global growth of aquaculture.

Aquaculture has been practiced for more than a century in the United States, although most of the growth of the U.S. aquaculture industry has occurred over the past two decades. The U.S. aquaculture industry, ranked ninth in the world in value of its aquaculture products ($685,970,000), is the fastest growing component of U.S. agriculture, accounting for nearly 181,000 jobs. In terms of economic importance, the aquaculture industry is comparable in value to the sheep industry and equivalent to either 18% of the swine industry or 30% of the turkey industry. Despite . . . industry growth, fish farming . . . accounts for only approximately 15% of U.S. fish and shellfish harvests.

Post–World War II seafood consumption in the United States has increased 52% on a per capita basis and 203% in total pounds consumed per year. The average American ate 14.8 lb of aquatic food in 1996. The United States, which imports over 60% of its fish and shellfish, is the world's second largest importer of seafood products, resulting in a U.S. annual seafood trade deficit slightly over $4.4 billion.

Global seafood demand is expected to grow by 70% in the next 35 years as the global population increases. At the same time, worldwide wild catches of many fish species are declining or have leveled off at maximum sustainable yield. For example, the near collapse in the stocks of cod, halibut, and a number of other species has caused the U.S. and Canadian governments to impose severe harvesting cutbacks in the Georges Bank fishing area of the northern Atlantic. As a result, the United States and Canada have placed increased priority on cultivating these species. To meet worldwide seafood demand, it is projected that aquaculture production will have to increase sevenfold, from 11 to 77 million metric tons by the year 2025.

The Environmental Impacts of Aquaculture

As a result of its rapid expansion in the [1990s], aquaculture . . . faces several significant policy issues that will influence the industry's development into the next century. D.W. Floyd, R.M. Sullivan, R.L. Ventrees, and C.F. Cole (1991) suggest that private production from publicly regulated resources, a common situation in aquaculture, is often a source of regulatory tension. For example, aquaculture firms are critically dependent on high-quality water, a publicly regulated resource. Often, the species raised in aquaculture facilities have been traditionally considered wildlife, another area of public regulation.

C. Tisdell (1995, 389) has noted that aquaculture "can sometimes be environmentally destructive, result in declining productivity and can threaten biodiversity." In aquaculture, as in land-based agriculture, externalities are often of a diffused type. They occur across a broad band or from many different points, especially when a number of farmers are sharing the same water body. Possible environmental externalities or spillovers from aquaculture include loss of habitat for recreational species and uses because space is allocated for aquaculture, the spread of diseases or pests to wild stocks, the reduction of wild stocks because of competition for areas or food sources, genetic dilution or displacement of native species from escapements from aquaculture facilities, land subsidence or saltwater intrusion from use of underground water, surface-water contamination, hypernutrification and eutrophication from nitrates or chemicals used in aquaculture, sedimentation and obstruction of water flows, coastal erosion from tree clearing, and increased resistance of bacteria and other diseases organisms from widespread use of antibiotics or other pharmaceuticals.

Traditional U.S. Environmental Management

The primary purpose of environmental laws is to protect the integrity of our natural resources. Most environmental laws operate by identifying resources to be protected, and then placing restrictions on what can be discharged into the protected resources. The laws usually identify the types of conduct known to affect the resource and place restrictions on those activities. Although there are numerous instruments for environmental management, U.S. environmental management has traditionally been based on direct regulation, a regulatory approach known as command and control. Rules, guidelines, and penalties are the main instruments used by regulatory agencies to protect and restore the environment.

World Aquacultural Production by Principal Producers in 1998

Country	1998 Production (thousand tons)	Value (U.S. $ thousands)
China	20,795	21,716
India	2,030	2,223
Japan	767	3,062
Indonesia	697	2,138
Bangladesh	584	1,494
Thailand	570	1,807
Viet Nam	522	1,349
United States	445	781
Norway	409	1,134
Korea Republic	327	544
Spain	314	282
Philippines	312	598
Chile	293	971
France	274	614
Italy	247	470
Other	2,279	7,900
World Total	**30,863**	**47,081**

UN FAO, "Yearbook of Fisheries Statistics: Aquaculture Production," 2000.

The most common command and control regulatory method is to require parties to obtain permits before engaging in a designated activity. Use of environmental regulation through permit and approval systems enables regulatory agencies to control the disturbance and degradation of the environment caused by human activities. N.D. Hamilton (1992) suggests that by imposing a requirement to obtain a permit, the public has the opportunity to set minimum standards for performance, which must be satisfied before the permit will be granted. Standards may be framed in terms of effluent emissions, ambient concentrations, or technological specifications. Setting standards also requires the establishment of a monitoring agency, which has the power to impose penalties for nonadherence. K. Reichelderfer and R. Kramer (1993) note that the federal approach to environmental regulation has been characterized by an absolute restriction of practices judged to pose unreasonable risks to consumers, regardless of geographic location, and provision to states of budgetary incentives to independently design programs that achieve broadly specified federal standard criteria.

States have increasingly enacted different environmental laws to protect the resources most important in the states and to regulate the types of economic activity found there. There are similarities between state environmental laws and common elements of how the laws work. Hamilton has identified the following steps typically found in a state environmental regulatory system:

1. State environmental law authorizes regulatory program.
2. State establishes an environmental protection agency.
3. Citizen commission establishes environmental policy.
4. Agency implements environmental laws.
5. Agency investigates complaints of pollution.
6. State takes legal action to enforce environmental law.

C.S. Russell (1993) examined the problem of enforcement and administration of regulations, suggesting that evidence points to widespread violations of permits in the case of conventional waste. He suggests that the violations are not due to a lack of technical ability or information, but rather to a failure to allocate sufficient resources to monitoring and enforcement. Regulation for environmental management relies on the centralization of large quantities of information, within few regulators. This information is costly and often impossible to gather. In addition, regulations are often overly broad in scope for an industry that varies widely from location to location, resulting further in uneven administration and enforcement. Consequently, lawmakers and economists have considered alternative environmental management strategies that rely on market-based solutions rather than regulation.

Alternative Instruments for Environmental Management

Policymakers have an array of instruments at their disposal to control environmental externalities. The . . . debate over environmental regulatory policy increasingly focuses on the form that government intervention should take, and in particular on the choice between direct regulations and economic or market-based instruments. One approach to environmental protection that is generating much interest is known as an economic incentives approach to environmental control. Contrary to command and control regulation, this approach, also known as free-market environmentalism or incentive-based environmental management, can make economic development the vehicle by which greater environmental protection is achieved.

The economic incentives approach uses a basic economic tenet that "incentives matter." People, in their own self-interest, do respond to incentives. According to T.H. Tietenberg (1992), good stewardship of the environment depends on how well social institutions harness self-interest through individual incentives. This approach achieves objectives by changing the economic incentives of the agents.

The specific environmental management instruments used within the free-market environmentalism approach are called incentive-based mechanism (IBM) or market-based incentives. These mechanisms can take many forms, but either rely on the "polluter pays" principle or provide economic compensation to elicit a targeted environmental behavior. Market-based instruments provide continuing incentives for polluters to search for cost-minimizing ways of abating pollution and, in this sense, are technologically dynamic.

The Classes of Market-Based Incentives

There are four general classes of economic or market-based incentive instruments: direct payment systems for adopting specific management practices (i.e., cost sharing, matching grants, subsidies); tradable pollution rights systems (i.e., tradable discharge permits, discharge reduction credits, waste deposit-refund system, habitat mitigation banking); environmental liability requirements (i.e., surety bonds, liability insurance); and special fees, taxes, or assessments, with receipts used for environmental or natural resource programs.

The market-based instruments frequently used to control environmental externalities are tradable emission permits or quotas, and Pigovian taxes that polluters pay per unit of emissions. Economists and environmental groups have stressed that environmental quality standards can be achieved by using marketable permits or emissions charges, but at a lower total cost. Tradable permits are based on a system of emission permits or quotas issued to polluters. Initially, these permits can either be distributed among participants or sold at auction to the highest bidders. These permits are freely tradable, and in principle can be bought and sold at the going market price. The pollution standard is therefore determined by the supply of pollution permits, which can be easily adjusted. One advantage of permit systems is that the initial distribution of permits can be tailored to greatly reduce the cost of the program to dischargers compared with a program of pollution charges. One noted drawback to marketable permits lies in the initial assignment of property rights to the environment. By distributing an initial number of permits among existing firms, a regulatory agency can make it more difficult for new firms to enter the industry, in effect creating barriers to entry and reducing competitiveness in the industry.

An optimal pollution tax or charge obliges the polluter to pay the full cost of the environmental services they consume and will be set equal to marginal damage costs at the optimal externality load. "Faced with emission charges or the price of emission credits, the cost-minimizing firm will seek ways to reduce pollution—either via output reductions, investments in clean-up activities or new technologies," A. Markandya and J. Richardson maintain. While the cost efficiency characteristic of market-based instruments is very powerful, several potential difficulties arise with market-based solutions for aquaculture environmental management.

Taxes or fees can be levied on fish farming practices that have harmful side effects, to induce farmers to switch to a substitute practice or cut back on the harmful activity. However, there are two possible problems with this approach: First, the government needs to exactly know the harmful effects caused by the practice. Second, for most practices, environmental damage varies from one region or site to another. "A tax or fee is simply too blunt an instrument," B.L. Gardner (1993) writes. Contracts for reduced discharges would be complex and difficult to monitor. The funds necessary to buy individuals' actions might be impossible to appropriate in stringent budgetary times. Gardner further suggests that the contribution a typical fish farmer makes to these problems may be too small to be worth the transaction cost of setting up, monitoring, and enforcing compliance with their provisions.

Gardner interjects a necessary caveat into the discussion of economic and market-based incentive-based mechanisms by suggesting that, while there should be room for innovative, market-based approaches in environmental regulation, this approach should not be considered a panacea. "There exists no way of turning the sour medicine of regulation into a tasty repast for the agricultural economy. Under any method of implementation, large costs are inevitable. . . ."

Environmental Laws and Regulations Affecting Aquaculture

The development of aquaculture and recognition of its potentially negative environmental impacts have resulted in increased levels of environmental regulations and resulting enforcement activities. However, legal and regulatory obstacles are commonly cited as major impediments to U.S. aquaculture growth and development. In addition to the regulations that all businesses are subject to, such as tax laws, labor regulations, and construction and land use controls, aquaculture operations are subject to regulation by numerous agencies at every level of government that have been delegated the legal authority of ensuring the protection of natural resources, as well as the public interest in those resources.

The diversity of agencies with jurisdiction over the industry is due in part to the nature of the industry. Aquaculture operations make use of natural resources and the public resources of coastal waters and submerged lands. In cases where aquaculture involves production, processing, and distribution of food for human consumption, a number of government entities at the federal, state, and local levels are involved in the regulation of the industry. When an aquaculture product is destined for export, regulations of other countries can also have an influence on the industry.

In many states, regulation of aquaculture has evolved in state game and fish departments that are oriented toward production and protection of game species for recreational purposes, rather than toward food production. Additional jurisdiction often resides in state environmental protection and health departments. State agencies and regulations often mirror their federal counterparts. . . .

Benefits for All

According to the Joint Subcommittee on Aquaculture (1993), the benefits to society as well as to the aquaculture industry will be maximized by the development of "rational" approaches to permitting, licensing, and regulatory requirements mandated by local, state, and federal statutes. . . .

The economic risks of overly rigid regulation and the uncertainty of benefits argue for consideration of economic and market-based incentive mechanisms, rather than regulatory mandates. In addition, the existing system of command and control regulation has led to a great deal of "ill will" between regulators and the aquaculture industry in some states. The alternative economic incentives approach offers a practical way to achieve environmental goals more flexibly and at a lower cost to society than traditional regulatory actions. It has been argued by T.H. Tietenberg (1998) and others that dollars spent to comply with environmental rules and regulations would have a greater impact if used to provide economic incentives. . . .

Despite their theoretical appeal and the potential savings they can generate, the effective application of incentive-based mechanisms is still very limited in U.S. aquaculture. . . . State governments have been slow to integrate market-based economic instruments into their aquaculture industry environmental management package. As the aquaculture industry continues its expansion, the industry will continue to focus on the effect of environmental regulations on profit. Simultaneously, interests concerned with the impact of policy on the environment will focus their attention on the environmental management of the aquaculture industry. This research finds the aquaculture industry poised in many respects to make the move to market-based environmental regulation, a move that may provide a management approach agreeable and beneficial to both interests.

Periodical Bibliography

The following articles have been selected to supplement the diverse views presented in this chapter.

Beth Baker — "Individual Fishing Quotas—A Complex and Contentious Issue," *BioScience*, March 1999.

Robert C. Cowen — "Giving Wild Fish a Break," *Christian Science Monitor*, May 3, 2001.

Gary E. Davis — "Seeking Sanctuaries," *National Parks*, November 1998.

Hannah Gillelan — "Homeless Fish: Bottom Trawls Bulldoze Seafloor Habitat," *Wild Earth*, Winter 2002/2003.

Rebecca J. Goldburg, Mathew S. Elliott, and Rosamond L. Naylor — "Marine Aquaculture in the United States," *Pew Oceans Commission*, 2001.

Greenpeace — "Freedom from Factory Trawlers?" *Greenpeace Magazine*, Summer 1998.

Ken Hinman — "Boosting Public Awareness of Fish," *Salt Water Sportsman*, March 2001.

Arthur Jones — "Consumers Can Help End Crisis in Oceans," *National Catholic Reporter*, May 8, 1998.

A.V. Krebs — "Fishing for Profits: The Grim Reaper Casts His Net," *Progressive Populist*, September 1998.

Harold Mooney — "When Fish Disappear," *Scientist*, June 21, 1999.

Rosamond L. Naylor, Susan L. Williams, and Donald R. Strong — "Aquaculture—A Gateway for Exotic Species," *Science*, November 23, 2001.

Robert Repetto — "A New Approach to Managing Fisheries," *Issues in Science and Technology*, Fall 2001.

Carl Safina — "Scorched-Earth Fishing," *Issues in Science and Technology*, Spring 1998.

Crystal Schaeffer — "Aquaculture: Factory Farms for Fish," *AV*, Summer 1998.

Samuel Scott — "Hunters or Shepherds of the Sea?" *Dollars & Sense*, January 2001.

Gerald Smith — "Distortion of World Fisheries by Capital," *Wild Earth*, Winter 2002/2003.

J.H. Tidwell and G.L. Allan — "Fish as Food: Aquaculture's Contribution," *EMBO Reports*, 2001.

CHAPTER 4

What Impact Do Human Activities Have on Marine Mammals?

Chapter Preface

Pollution of the marine environment is one of several human activities that has an impact on marine mammals. In early 1988 nearly twenty-five thousand harbor seals in the North and Baltic Seas—60 to 70 percent of the population—abruptly died of a distemper virus. The seals' deaths appeared to be part of a disturbing trend. In the late 1970s an influenza virus killed 450 harbor seals off the coast of Cape Cod, Massachusetts. During 1987 and 1988 the morbillivirus killed about 750 bottlenose dolphins along beaches from New Jersey to Florida. Studies revealed that the bodies of these marine mammals contained high levels of persistent organic pollutants (POPs) that are found in a wide variety of industrial chemicals, pesticides, herbicides, and manufacturing byproducts. These pollutants are called persistent because they do not decompose easily and once released into the environment last a long time.

When POPs accumulate in an animal's body, they act as endocrine disruptors, which interfere with the hormones that facilitate the growth and operation of critical systems in the body. Endocrine disruptors can have lifelong effects on the skeleton, brain, and the immune system. These compounds can leave an animal prone to developmental abnormalities and can disrupt its ability to produce antibodies or T-cells, making it vulnerable to infections. This vulnerability, researchers claim, explains why so many seals and dolphins were unable to combat the viruses that ultimately killed them.

POPs become concentrated in animals higher up the food chain by a process known as bioaccumulation. These pollutants are lipophilic, which means that they attach to the fatty tissue of animals. When POPs enter the marine environment, they are ingested by invertebrates. Fish then eat the invertebrates and are subsequently eaten by larger fish, which eventually are eaten by marine mammals. According to environmental journalist Michael A. Rivlin, "A killer whale at the top of the food chain retains in its body contaminants that may have been distilled 10 million times."

Ironically, the man-made pollutants that threaten marine

mammals also threaten the human animal. "Seals and other marine mammals, poisoned by chemicals produced by people, are sometimes hunted and eaten by other people," Rivlin explains. Many Inuit, tribes who occupy the Arctic regions, depend on meat and blubber from marine mammals for their survival. Eric Dewailly, a community health worker, examined POP levels in Quebec, Canada, in the mid-1980s. By going into a remote northern region of the province, he hoped to find an isolated population of Arctic Inuit to compare with people who lived farther south, whom he assumed would experience higher levels of POP contamination due to their proximity to urban centers. To his surprise, he found that the breast milk of Inuit mothers contained five times the amount of polychlorinated biphenyls (PCBs)—one of the most well known of the POPs—as the breast milk of southern women. According to Dewailly, "a sugar cube-sized piece of muktuk—the skin and surface fat from the beluga—contains the accepted maximum weekly limit of PCBs." Some Inuit, he claims, eat a hundred times that amount in a week. What he found most disturbing was that Inuit babies developed twenty times more infectious diseases during their first year than babies in southern Quebec. Infants with the highest exposure were almost twice as likely as unexposed children to develop acute inner-ear infections. As a result, nearly one in four Inuit teenagers has long-term partial hearing loss.

The problem of marine pollution remains the subject of debate. The authors of the viewpoints in the following chapter examine the impact of other human activities on marine mammals.

"Commercial whaling cannot be conducted on a sustainable basis."

The Ban on Commercial Whaling Protects Endangered Whales

Greenpeace

Because the environmental and economic conditions that brought whales to the brink of extinction in the twentieth century have not changed, argues Greenpeace in the following viewpoint, replacing the ban on commercial whaling with a scheme to manage whale hunting will seriously threaten whale populations. According to Greenpeace, an international environmental organization, commercial whaling is motivated by the desire for profit, not preservation. Even with the ban, Greenpeace claims, some whaling nations have falsified records and manipulated quotas to increase the number of whales they are allowed to kill, practices that are likely to increase if the ban is lifted. The International Whaling Commission rejected revised management schemes proposed at its May 2002 meeting.

As you read, consider the following questions:

1. According to Greenpeace, what biological characteristics do whales have that make it impossible for them to recover quickly from overexploitation?
2. What did IFAW researchers discover when analyzing the DNA of samples purchased in various whale markets, according to Greenpeace?

D espite a history of repeated failure to control commercial whaling under a succession of management regimes, the International Whaling Commission (IWC) is currently in the process of developing a new set of rules, known as the Revised Management Scheme or RMS, which could be used to manage commercial whaling operations at some point in the near future and, if agreed, could herald the lifting of the moratorium on all commercial whaling.[1]

Greenpeace believes that whatever provisions might be included in any future RMS, they would not be sufficient to ensure the adequate protection of the world's remaining whales. This briefing sets out the reasons why commercial whaling cannot be conducted on a sustainable basis.

Failing to Manage the Seas

There are a number of factors both biological and economic which explain why commercial whaling inevitably led to the depletion of whale populations in the past (see Greenpeace briefing 'What's wrong with whaling' December 2001). These factors have not changed, and there is a growing body of evidence to suggest that the continuing degradation of the world's oceans, through climate change, ozone depletion, toxic and noise pollution and prey depletion as a result of over-fishing, are all threatening the health of whale populations.

Fisheries management regimes have largely been failures, often leading to the demise of the fisheries they were intended to protect. From the North Sea to the Grand Banks of Newfoundland and around the world, we have seen the collapse of commercial fisheries despite the science based management schemes that were designed with the objective of ensuring that the fisheries were sustainable.

Given this inability to manage fisheries, it is unwise for the IWC to think that it can manage whaling, when whales are inherently more vulnerable to commercial exploitation than most fish species. This is a consequence of their very different biology. Most fish reproduce by releasing huge

1. The members of the International Whaling Commission (IWC) voted to reject the revised management scheme (RMS) proposals submitted by Japan and Sweden at the IWC's May 2002 meeting in Shimonoseki, Japan.

numbers of eggs into the water. Most do not survive, but as long as there are good conditions for the young fish to grow, the eggs from a small percentage of the population can quickly regenerate the whole population. In contrast, whales have only a single offspring at a time which needs at least a year of maternal care before it can survive on its own and many years before it can reproduce. As a result of these biological characteristics, whales can never recover quickly from overexploitation.

Despite all the evidence to the contrary, the whaling countries, Japan and Norway, continue to claim that things are different now and that commercial whaling could be conducted without depleting whale populations. However, there is little to suggest that Japan and Norway are either interested in sustainability or prepared to abide with any future RMS.

Examining Market Forces

The commercial whaling industry is a profit driven industry: put simply, the more whales you catch, the more money you make. It is hard to predict exactly how the market would behave were commercial whaling to be made legitimate again, but it is certain that the industry would press for even greater quotas. Already Norwegian whalers are calling for hunts of up to 3,000 minkes per year and for quotas of fin whales. Japan expanded its North Pacific hunt to include sperm and Bryde's whales and describes the hunt as 'a feasibility study', The implication is clear: it wants to kill whales in increasing numbers and it wants to expand the number of species it targets.

Furthermore, there is no reason to believe that the industry could be confined to the 2 countries currently whaling. At [the July 2001] IWC, Iceland tried to rejoin the IWC with the express intent of resuming commercial whaling. Iceland's reasons for rejoining are purely commercial, in that it thinks the IWC may soon agree to allow commercial whaling and that the international trade in whale products will also resume. Iceland's whaling has always been an export oriented industry. Iceland has also expressed interest in targeting species other than minkes. Korea and Russia are also likely candidates to try and cash in on the commercial opportunities if there is a resumption of whaling.

The Incentive to Cheat

Cheating both under and outside the IWC has always characterised the whaling industry. The whaling industry has a shameful history of large-scale organised cheating. For instance, in 1994 it was finally revealed how the Soviet whaling fleet had, over the course of 40 years, systematically carried out the falsification of catch records. Some of this cheating had occurred when there were Japanese observers onboard. For instance, for the 1961/2 season the Soviets claimed that their four whaling fleets had only killed 270 humpback whales, but in reality one fleet had killed 1,568 in total.

[In 2001] came the astonishing account by Mr. [Isao] Kondo, a former executive of Nihon Hogei K.K. (Japan Whaling Co. Ltd), detailing the various methods used to manipulate catch data by the Japanese coastal whaling stations right up until the moratorium. This included converting the catches of undersized sperm whales to fewer large whales, stretching the measurements of undersized whales and mis-reporting the sex of female sperm whales. Sometimes inspectors would be taken out to dinner when these illegal activities were taking place.

Mr. Kondo revealed that coastal whalers catching the most valuable species, the Bryde's whale, went over their quotas year after year and falsified their catch reports, until the moratorium stopped their whaling. The false reports were forwarded to the IWC by the government of Japan. These false reports would have increased any future quotas set under the RMS, but the government of Japan took no action to correct them.

The Problem of Pirate Whaling

There is also the very real threat of pirate whaling. Before the moratorium, the market for whale products and the high price of whale meat and blubber provided the incentives for opportunists to whale outside the system—a practice known as pirate whaling. Pirate whalers did not respect whether a whale was from an endangered or more abundant population, the larger the species the more profit per whale. This approach to whaling is exactly what led to the present situation whereby the world's largest whales were hunted to the verge of extinction first.

Only a matter of time

Renault. © by Rothco. Reprinted with permission.

We already have evidence of current illegal whaling. Testing samples of whale meat on sale in Japan has found meat from endangered species such as humpback and gray whales on sale. The gray whale products are likely to be from the western North Pacific population—one of the rarest whales in the world with only 100 or so individuals left. There are surprising amounts of meat from fin and sei whales on sale, even though legal imports of these species ended a decade ago.

Researchers working for IFAW [International Fund for Animal Welfare] purchased 129 samples from various whale markets. DNA analysis revealed that 100 of the samples were Minke whale, two were sperm whale and two were Bryde's—the three species for which Japan issues hunting permits. But of the other 25 samples, two were humpback, five were from fin whale, one was sei whale, fourteen were dolphin and one was *horse*.

Commercial whaling has proved uncontrollable in the past. There is no reason to believe that it is any more controllable now.

Although DNA testing is helpful in detecting illegal whale products, it doesn't provide a way to stop illegal trade.

The Uncertainty of Whale Science

The RMP [Revised Management Procedure], which is the model which would be used to calculate catch quotas under any agreed RMS, although intended to be precautionary is not necessarily foolproof. All models are a simplification of the real world and may not reflect the reality of environmental fluctuations on whale populations. The model also relies on population estimates but as ever these are problematic due to the inherent difficulties in counting whales accurately. Most counts are done by the whalers themselves.

Also, the model requires a catch history and, as we have seen, the whalers sometimes conceal their catches which has the effect of increasing any quotas calculated using the RMP.

Even the estimated number of North Atlantic minkes, the population of whales targeted by Norway and one of the most studied populations of whales in the world, is uncertain. The IWC Scientific Committee currently accepts 2 different population estimates as being valid for use in the RMP. These are 118,000 and an earlier figure of 67,500 based on a survey conducted in 1989.

There is massive uncertainty as to the number of minkes in the Southern Ocean too.

Considering Environmental Threats

With each passing year, the evidence that whales are at risk from changes in their ocean environment grows ever larger.

This is by itself a good reason not to repeat the dangerous experiment of allowing commercial whaling. Known environmental threats to whales include climate change, pollution, overfishing, ozone depletion, capture in fishing nets and even ship strikes.

At [the 2002] IWC the Scientific Committee was unable to agree a number for the Southern Ocean minkes. The figure of 760,000 as used by Japan to justify its whaling for the last 10 years is no longer valid and the new estimate could be less than half of this because recent counts indicate much smaller numbers. A number of reasons have been given as to why the new estimate is so much lower than the old, including the hypothesis that the Southern Ocean minkes may have suffered a major decline as a result of climate change.

Perhaps most disturbing of all the information to come out of [2002's] meeting of the IWC Scientific Committee was a report on the situation of the western North Pacific gray whales. This population, hunted almost to the verge of extinction in the early part of last century, now only numbers around 100 individuals of which only 12 are calf bearing females. [In 2002] some have been found to be emaciated with their bones showing through their blubber. For some reason these whales are not getting enough of the benthic organisms that constitute their prey and this may be due to increased sea temperatures. Despite this, seismic testing is being conducted in their feeding grounds in the search for new oil and gas reserves. That these critically endangered whales may actually be pushed into extinction is an indication of just how far we have degraded the whales' ocean habitats.

Changing the Rules

The whaling nations will always bend the rules to suit their purposes.

A telling example of this is how in 2001 Norway changed the way it calculated its catch quotas. Norway claims that it calculates its catch quotas according to the provisions set out in the Revised Management Procedure or RMP. The RMP is the mathematical model devised by the IWC which would be used to calculate catch quotas if the moratorium were to be lifted. However when Norway realised that if it was to follow the RMP exactly using the IWC agreed tuning level (the tuning level is the % of the pristine population that would be left after 100 years of operating the RMP) it would only have a quota of about 300 whales, it decided to use a lower tuning level so that the quota would be increased. Norway's quota with the lower tuning level was 580 minke whales.

In July 2001 the Fisheries Agency of Japan (FAJ) changed the law regarding whales caught as bycatch (i.e. whales which get entangled in fishing nets). Under the old regulations fishermen were obliged to release live whales accidentally captured in fishing gear, but now fishermen are allowed to land the whales and sell the meat, providing they report the catch and take a DNA sample. Figures just released show that 52 whales have been caught since the legislation was changed compared with between 20 and 30 whales a year reported beforehand. This change in regulation by the FAJ is widely perceived as an underhand way of increasing the annual whale catch. . . .

The Future of Whaling and Whales

If the IWC agrees and adopts a RMS into the IWC schedule there will be enormous pressure to lift the moratorium on commercial whaling.

Once the moratorium is lifted it is only a matter of time before the whaling industry ensures that the provisions in the RMS that limit their profitability (i.e. provisions intended to safeguard the whales) are eroded. New countries are likely to start whaling and there will be a marked increase in pirate whaling.

The 20th century saw the greatest devastation of whale populations in history but it also saw recognition of our mistakes. Now the lessons of history are being ignored and the 21st century is likely to see the resumption of factory ship whaling worldwide.

"To Japan and other countries, a Western antagonism to whaling and to the use of whale products smacks of cultural imperialism."

The Ban on Commercial Whaling Is Unnecessary and Unfair

William Aron, William Burke, and Milton Freeman

In the following viewpoint William Aron, William Burke, and Milton Freeman claim that the International Whaling Commission (IWC) was established to regulate commercial whaling, not ban it. Efforts by nations morally opposed to commercial whaling to impose a ban on whaling violate international law and risk antagonizing whaling nations, the authors maintain. Moreover, they argue, scientific evidence shows that sustainable whaling is possible and indicates that not all whales are in danger of extinction. Aron, former director of the Alaska Fisheries Science Center, is a professor at the University of Washington. Burke is a professor of law and marine affairs at the University of Washington, and Freeman is professor of anthropology at the University of Alberta.

As you read, consider the following questions:

1. In the authors' opinion, why has the International Whaling Commission dragged out negotiations over monitoring and enforcing the Revised Management Procedure?
2. What species of whales do the authors maintain are in no danger of extinction?

William Aron, William Burke, and Milton Freeman, "Flouting the Convention," *Atlantic Monthly*, vol. 283, May 1999, pp. 22–29. Copyright © 1999 by William Aron, William Burke, and Milton Freeman. Reproduced by permission.

In 1946 a fifteen-year effort by whaling nations to exert multilateral control over the whaling industry finally produced the International Convention for the Regulation of Whaling, the fundamental purpose of which was "to provide for the proper conservation of whale stocks and thus make possible the orderly development of the whaling industry." The convention established the fourteen-nation IWC [International Whaling Commission], which was empowered to regulate the industry but was granted no authority to amend the convention itself. In adopting, revising, or terminating regulations the IWC is required always to follow the convention's intent—namely, as explicitly stated in Article V, "to provide for the conservation, development, and optimum utilization of the whale resources," taking into consideration "the interests of the consumers of whale products and the whaling industry." Simply put, no possible interpretation of the convention allows for putting an end to whaling when credible scientific opinion supports the sustainable use of abundant whale resources.

The Efforts to Manage Whaling

The IWC started off badly. For nearly thirty years after its inception it tolerated whaling at unsustainable levels. Many of the largest species declined so precipitously that in 1972 the United States began calling for a ten-year moratorium on all commercial whaling. The proposal was intended to shock the IWC into getting its house in order—that is, putting into effect a management system that would both maintain the whaling industry and allow whale populations to recover. When the moratorium was voted down in 1972 and 1973, activists threatened to boycott goods from whaling nations; targets included Russian vodka, Japanese cameras and TV sets, and Norwegian and Icelandic fish products. The whaling industry was forced to compromise.

In 1974 the IWC endorsed the New Management Procedure [NMP]—an Australian plan, with strong backing from the United States, that essentially banned whaling of all overexploited stocks but permitted commercial catches of abundant stocks at levels that would not threaten their existence. The plan satisfied the IWC Scientific Committee, most of whose members had objected both to the excessive size of the earlier whale quotas and to the idea of a moratorium on commercial whaling, which they also viewed as excessive. The NMP took effect in the 1975–1976 whaling season. Since then not one whale population has been jeopardized by a commercial whaling operation. . . .

In 1994 the RMP [Revised Management Procedure]—a risk-averse successor to a management scheme that had already proved successful by terminating the harvest of all whales in jeopardy—was accepted in principle by the commission. In practice, however, the IWC has yet to allow a return to commercial whaling; instead it has deliberately dragged out negotiations over monitoring and enforcing the RMP. By focusing on increasingly arcane questions of logistics, costs, and methodology, each needing lengthy debate, the anti-whaling majority has successfully pushed the target for the whaling nations ever further into the future—a procedure that has been likened to moving the goal posts.

A Bitter Standoff

The cause of this charade is obvious: a majority of the IWC wants to halt all commercial whaling, no matter what the convention says. Indeed, Australia, Great Britain, New Zealand, and the United States—and, more recently, Austria and Italy—have explicitly stated that they will not approve commercial whaling under any conditions. In 1991 the Australian commissioner stated flatly that there was no longer any need to hunt "such large and beautiful animals" for food. Conceding that no scientific reason exists to ban all whaling, the U.S. commissioner announced in 1991 that he would defend the U.S. position on ethical grounds.

Such an approach, based on moral judgments rather than science, plainly violates both the convention and the international rule of law. And because anti-whaling activists will accept nothing less than a total ban, they leave no room for good-faith negotiation and compromise. The whaling industry will not cooperate in its own elimination, nor will the governments of whaling nations permit their citizens to be victimized. As a result, scientists, whalers, and activists are locked in a never-ending battle. The bitter standoff violates international law, fosters tensions between otherwise friendly nations, and undermines environmental legislation. Worst of all, the cynical actions of the IWC's anti-whaling majority constitute a clear warning to all nations engaged in negotiating multilateral environmental agreements: Beware, for the United States and its allies may suddenly adopt new interpretations of long-standing principles, and use them against you. Even if you accept treaties, these countries may (for purely domestic reasons) apply sanctions against you for actions fully in compliance with those treaties.

Not All Whales Are Endangered

Despite guidelines accompanying the International Convention for the Regulation of Whaling that refer to only twelve whale species (right, pigmy right, bowhead, humpback, blue, fin, Bryde's, minke, sei, sperm, and Arctic and Antarctic bottlenose), many IWC members act as if the convention covered all whales—and even all cetaceans, the order of eighty-three species of aquatic mammals that also includes dolphins and porpoises. Few scientists deny that several species of whale—including the blue, the right, the bowhead, and the humpback—have been severely overhunted by commercial whalers and are now properly regarded as endangered. But almost all scientists admit that most other species are in no danger of extinction Minke and pilot whales, for example, have populations of more than a million, and sperm whales have a population of about a million. Gray whales (probably more abundant now than ever) and some regional stocks of sei, Bryde's, and fin whales (less abundant than in earlier times, but not dramatically so) are in no sense endangered by controlled hunts.

Unsurprisingly, researchers continue to argue that endangered species should generally not be hunted. However, the IWC allows native peoples in Alaska and Siberia to hunt limited numbers of bowhead along with gray whales to meet their needs. Neither species has been adversely affected by such hunting. Estimates of the bowhead population in the late 1970s ranged from 500 to 2,000 animals; the current bowhead population is believed to exceed 8,000. The rise in the estimate is due in part to population growth but mostly to better survey techniques. It is estimated that the gray-whale population has increased from about 7,000 animals in the 1930s to more than 26,000 today, despite authorized subsistence catches of 140 or more a year. The difference is thought to reflect population growth.

Answering Objections to Sustainable Whaling

Just because it is possible to harvest whales without placing their populations in jeopardy does not mean that the practice is acceptable. Whale protectionists often claim that whales are extremely intelligent—as smart as, if not smarter than, humankind—and that the killing of such highly sentient creatures is wrong. But whales have been studied intensively for decades, and there is still no strong evidence that they are uniquely intelligent. Many species throughout the animal kingdom demonstrate behaviors and abilities just as complex as those demonstrated by whales.

Sustainable Use Maintains Balance in Nature

We have an important responsibility which is to help maintain the BALANCE IN NATURE. One of the most important elements used to maintain the balance is sustainable utilization. Everything is INTER-CONNECTED.

When one component in the web of life is over exploited and then protected, the balance in nature is lost and all living creatures suffer. An example of this is in the Antarctic where there is concern over the Blue Whales. People do not know that there are over 1 million minke whales who are consuming the vast majority of the food which leaves the blue whales in a precarious situation. If you want the blue whales to increase then you need to cull some of the minke whales.

Tom Mexsis Happynook, *Times Colonists*, September 28, 1998.

Another major objection to whaling is that it is an inhumane practice carried out unnecessarily. Let us be clear: "humane killing" is an oxymoron. The best we can hope for in killing animals is that death be as quick and as nearly painless as possible. Experience has shown that in the whaling industry this is largely achieved—just as it is in the food industries that kill millions of cattle, sheep, pigs, and chickens every day.

Some whaling-ban advocates feel that whaling has no place in the contemporary world. They point to the fact that many industrialized countries, despite having engaged in commercial whaling twenty or thirty years ago, are now fervent opponents of whaling. If this is the case, the advocates ask, why should Norway and Japan and a few other countries continue whaling? The trouble is that this argument assumes that there are no fundamental cultural differences between whaling and nonwhaling societies: the former are simply considered to be stuck at an earlier stage of development, in need of being goosed up the ladder of progress.

Anthropologists believe otherwise. The societies that have abandoned whaling hunted whales principally for oil. Until the late 1960s whale oil was used for many purposes—in submarine guidance systems, for example, leading the Pentagon to object to listing sperm whales as an endangered species. Indeed, the IWC was established in part to ensure the profitability of the whale-oil business, which it did by setting quotas measured in units of oil. When substitutes for whale oil became available in the 1970s, nations that whaled primarily for oil stopped hunting whales.

Respecting Different Cultures

Things were different in other nations, especially Norway and Japan, where whaling is an ancient occupation worthy of the respect and support that Americans award to, say, the running of a farm. Norwegians view whaling as part of the hard, honorable life of a fisherman—a reliable slow-season activity that helps fishing communities to make it through the year. The Japanese who come from a long line of whalers have deeply held moral beliefs about maintaining their family tradition. To be prevented from honoring their ancestors in this manner is a source of shame. After the 1982 moratorium some Norwegian fishers went bankrupt. The same thing happened in Iceland. Given the abundance of the whale stocks, these nations ask, why can't such people be free to practice their traditional livelihood? Anthropologists have long observed the primary role played by traditional foods in the social structure and moral norms of a community—a role that is captured in the widely repeated aphorism "you are what you eat." Asking people to give up their customary diet is in many ways like asking them to give up part of their identity.

The Japanese are particularly angered by the IWC's ongoing failure to fulfill its legal obligations to whaling-treaty members. They point to the extensive research—much of it done by non-Japanese scientists and endorsed by the IWC Scientific Committee and the international scientific community—suggesting that an interim reinstatement of coastal minke whaling (until the implementation of the RMP) would not be harmful. When such research is ignored or trivialized by the IWC itself, it is easy for the Japanese to conclude that the United States and its anti-whaling allies are irrational, dishonorable, and racially prejudiced. To Japan and other countries, a Western antagonism to whaling and to the use of whale products smacks of cultural imperialism.

The Tactics of Whaling Ban Activists

To counter the pleas of countries like Norway and Japan, the anti-whaling members of the IWC assert that worldwide public opinion now opposes commercial whaling. But the convention's acceptance of whaling is not an isolated anachronism. . . . United Nations conferences have twice had an opportunity to oppose whaling, and have twice declined to take it. In 1982, soon after the IWC adopted the whaling moratorium, 119 states signed the UN Convention on the Law of the Sea, an agreement that permits whaling on the high seas. Individual nations may forbid their nationals to take whales, and coastal states may prohibit all takes within their national waters, but unless states jointly agree otherwise, whaling can go on. In 1992 the UN Conference on Environment and Development reaffirmed the provisions of the Convention on the Law of the Sea, explicitly rejecting efforts by anti-whaling forces to exclude whales from the list of resources open to sustainable use and development. Both actions show that there is no international consensus against whaling. . . .

Perhaps sensing that informed public support for a total whaling ban would be weak, whaling-ban advocates frequently resort to campaigns that can most kindly be referred to as "artful." Despite a decades-old scientific consensus that most whale species do not face extinction, Greenpeace and other anti-whaling groups continue to decry a supposed illicit trade in whale products, implying that a large global market for such products exists. This has not been the case for decades, and is not likely to be so again. Nor are there large numbers of potential whaling interests anywhere in the world waiting to resume uncontrolled whaling once the moratorium is lifted, as whaling-ban advocates also claim. What is at work here is politics—and the opportunity for anti-whaling organizations to raise substantial revenues through emotionally powerful but deceptive campaigns.

The whaling industry has done much to deserve activists' ire, and public-awareness campaigns about its behavior are laudable. But they are also simplistic and misleading—often deliberately so, to attract funding and support. The slogan "Save the whale," for example, was far more effective in awakening public concern than the scientifically correct "Save the particular whale stocks threatened by overhunting" would have been. Unfortunately, the slogan was hijacked by a small group of animal-protection activists, who mustered public support for a whaling ban by creating the false impression that all whale stocks were in danger. Politicians found it easy to follow this lead. . . .

The Risks of Intransigence

In the ongoing campaign to ban whale hunting altogether, the ends do not justify the means. By spurning all attempts at compromise, today's anti-whaling crusaders have the potential to disrupt the large-scale environmental legislation of tomorrow.

To address such issues as global warming, the overuse of freshwater supplies, acid rain, overfishing in the oceans, the introduction of species to new environments, and other international environmental problems, the nations of the world will have to negotiate with one another—and for negotiations to be successful, *all* sides will have to compromise. Necessarily, the sacrifices will be harder for poor countries than for rich ones—note the reluctance of Third World nations to sign a greenhouse-gas agreement. But the sacrifices must be agreed upon and implemented in good faith. For

Western nations to provide clear evidence in a highly visible forum that they are willing to flout past agreements, as they have with whaling, dims the prospect for reaching new ones in the future.

Because of the intransigence of anti-whaling nations, the IWC is rapidly becoming irrelevant. Some nations that want to whale but view the commission as a science-free forum for eco-posturing—Japan and Norway in particular—have taken advantage of the convention's provisions for opting out of IWC decisions. Other whaling nations, such as Canada and Iceland, have simply exited the IWC. Today almost all whaling is conducted by nonmembers in accordance with general international law or by IWC members ignoring the commission's (nonbinding) decisions. Fortunately, the latter nations, mainly Norway and Japan, have chosen to limit their catches to sustainable levels. But the example of an international environmental agency politicizing itself into irrelevance is alarming.

A Plan for Controlled Whaling

The means for protecting whale populations, allowing a resumption of controlled whaling, and rescuing the IWC from itself already exist: a plan known as the Revised Management Scheme.[1] First proposed in 1992 by Australia, and supported by five other nations, including the United States, the Revised Management Scheme incorporates the Revised Management Procedure and adds an observer program and other safeguards to ensure that whaling operations do not endanger whale populations.

Under such a plan a return to large-scale commercial whaling is highly unlikely. The reasons are economic, biological, and social: Inexpensive substitutes have eliminated the market for whale oil, and the market for whale meat is very limited. The slow growth of whale populations means that large-scale whaling is unlikely even to be possible for the foreseeable future. And whales today are protected by the most important safeguard of all: an ecological awareness,

1. The members of the International Whaling Commission (IWC) voted to reject the Revised Management Scheme (RMS) proposals submitted by Japan and Sweden at the IWC's May 2002 meeting in Shimonoseki, Japan.

which is now firmly implanted in the minds of the public and politicians alike, that nowhere existed during the ruinous heyday of industrial whaling.

Pointing to the recently revealed cheating of the Soviet Antarctic whaling fleet, whaling-ban advocates claim that the ban can't be lifted because whaling nations can't be trusted. But the cheating took place before any observer program existed. Together with other enforcement methods, observer programs have proved effective in regulating the take of dolphins in the eastern tropical Pacific Ocean and of fish in the United States' exclusive economic zone of the North Pacific. An international observer program independent of the IWC was implemented [in 1998] by four North Atlantic whaling nations. But attempts to put together an observer program within the IWC are moving extremely slowly, because anti-whaling nations see that putting it in place will remove a barrier to whaling.

As a first step toward rescuing the International Whaling Commission, the Revised Management Scheme should be completed and fully implemented without further delay. Ending the charade at the IWC would induce more whaling countries to follow its dictates—and would for the first time bring most or all of the whaling industry under a science-based scheme of international regulation. It would also suggest that nations in diverse economic and cultural circumstances can cooperate and compromise for the mutual environmental good—something that will be in ever greater demand.

VIEWPOINT

"The U.S. Navy is . . . pursuing deployment of a secret submarine detection system that threatens to disrupt [whales' and dolphins'] acoustic ability."

Antisubmarine Sonar Threatens Marine Mammals

Nathan LaBudde

The U.S. Navy has been using low-frequency, high-decibel sonar to track hard-to-detect submarines despite the fact that these transmissions threaten to disrupt the acoustic abilities on which marine mammals depend, claims Nathan LaBudde in the following viewpoint. According to LaBudde, when the Navy conducted an environmental impact assessment on the Surveillance Towed Array Sonar System, Low Frequency Active (LFA), gray whales in the vicinity of the testing changed their migration pattern, and humpback whales stopped singing. Moreover, the sonar appeared to disorient mothers and calves, resulting in their separation. LaBudde argues that the Navy sees these as negligible short-term effects when they may in fact prove harmful in the long term. LaBudde is an environmentalist with the Earth Island Institute.

As you read, consider the following questions:

1. What example does LaBudde provide to show the role sound plays in the life of a marine mammal?
2. According to the author, what happened to humpback whales days after being exposed to high decibel explosions and drilling off Newfoundland in 1993?

Nathan LaBudde, "U.S. Navy Plans Ocean Assault," *Earth Island Journal*, vol. 41, Summer 1999, p. 18. Copyright © 1999 by *Earth Island Journal*. Reproduced by permission.

The oceans are vast, dark habitat for whales and dolphins who rely on sound much as people rely on sight to carry out their primary life functions, from communication to finding food and escaping danger. The US Navy is now pursuing deployment of a secret submarine detection system that threatens to disrupt these animals' acoustic ability.[1]

Detecting Phantom Enemies

The end of the Cold War brought a close to the US Navy's games of cat and mouse with Russian submarines. Today, the US is spending $64 billion to develop Virginia-class attack submarines to counter a phantom opponent.

The navy uses tactical formations of battleships, aircraft carriers, destroyers, and the like, called carrier groups. While carrier groups visiting ports of call around the world provide political benefits reminiscent of [Theodore] Roosevelt's Great White Fleet's, naval strategists fear that larger, slower vessels in coastal waters are vulnerable to new small, hard-to-detect submarines. Current passive detection technology is said to be inadequate. Enter Surveillance Towed Array Sonar System, Low Frequency Active (LFA), which blasts low-frequency (100–1000Hz) high-decibel noise and interprets the echoes. LFA sonar is of such a magnitude, 235dB [decibel] to 280dB, that any living thing—fish, sea turtles, marine mammals, humans—in the target area would likely find the noise lethal. Whales show an aversion to man-made sounds starting at 120dB, and the noise pain threshhold for whales may be 170dB at half a mile.

To begin understanding the role sound plays in the life of a marine mammal and why disruption is dangerous, one need only consider the following: For millions of years, populations of humpbacks have been singing similar songs to one another over thousands of miles of open ocean. Over a

1. On July 16, 2002, the U.S. Department of Defense authorized the U.S. Navy to employ the Surveillance Towed Array Sonar System, Low Frequency Active (LFA) under restrictions it believed would reduce adverse effects on the marine environment. On October 31, 2002, the U.S. District Court for the Northern District of California granted a preliminary injunction, ordering the Navy to cease employing LFA sonar. The court set a hearing for June 2003, during which the parties will have agreed on how LFA sonar can be used so that the impact on marine mammals is limited.

season, a distinct version of the humpback song is repeated. Parallel changes spread through the population until all are singing a new song.

Testing the Impact

From 1980–95 the Navy tested LFA for some 7,500 hours without regard for the United States' environmental laws. Pressure from environmental groups finally forced the Navy to undertake a field study in 1997–98 to comply with the Endangered Species Act, Marine Mammal Protection Act, and National Environmental Policy Act. It studied behavioral impacts on whales from a simulated LFA sound source for an environmental impact assessment (EIA) before authorizing four LFA ships (one is already under construction) and actual LFA deployment. The Navy hired two civilian whale acoustics experts, Dr. Christopher Clarke of Cornell University and Dr. Peter Tyack of Woods Hole Oceanographic Institute.

The initial phase studied blue and fin whales. For eight weeks the *Cory Chouest*, outfitted with a tower of underwater LFA "speakers," transmitted 140dB omni-directional sound pulses every eight seconds for ten minutes at a time, while aerial and shipboard spotters observed whale behavior over a 119-square-mile area. Observers weren't told when the LFA source was transmitting. The sample group was extremely small, during a season when most blue whales have gathered farther north. Tests were hampered by inclement weather and scratched test days. During the testing period a pod of forty fin whales was seen "racing across the surface of the water," an event previously unseen and unknown by veteran whale researchers. Blue whales' vocalizations decreased by half and fin whales' by a third when the sound was broadcast.

Phase two studied the effects of LFA sonar on California gray whales migrating to their birthing and wintering lagoons in Baja California. When the sound source was turned on, whales coming within six-tenths of a mile of the 185dB sound source moved as much as a mile laterally to avoid it. It remains to be seen how this disturbance, if made routine, would affect the gray whales' annual 5,000-mile migration, one of the longest of any animal on Earth.

U.S. Naval Exercises Using Low-Frequency Active Sonar

Exercise	Area of operations	Period of operations	Complied with Environmental law?
Magellan II	Classified; presumably the same area used in LFA-14	Aug. 1994	No
LFA-13	Gulf of Oman and Persian Gulf	Summer 1995	No
LFA-14 Northern	West of San Francisco Bay, extending north along the Mendocino coast	Sept. 26, 1995– Oct. 9, 1995	No
LFA-14 Southern	South of the Channel Islands, extending south along the Baja California coast	Sept. 26, 1995– Oct. 9, 1995	No
MARCOT 2-95	West of Vancouver Island (British Columbia)	Fall 1995	No
LFA-15	South of the Channel Islands, extending south along the Baja California coast	Feb. 1996– Mar. 1996	No
LFA-16 (RIMPAC-96)	Various sites around the Hawaiian Islands	May 1996– June 1996	No
CNO Project K 154-4	Southwest of Kodiak Island (Alaska), extending west across the Aleutian Islands	Aug. 12, 1997– Aug. 31, 1997	No

Natural Resources Defense Council, *Sounding the Depths: Supertankers, Sonar, and the Rise of Undersea Noise*, 1999.

Observing Unusual Behaviors

The final test was conducted in Hawai'ian waters north of Kona, on humpback whales. Four-fifths of singing humpback whales stopped singing when exposed to the sound. Many humpbacks left the test area during the experiment; one whale-watcher suspended operations for lack of humpbacks. During the month-long test period, members of the Hawai'i Ocean Mammal Institute documented instances of abandoned cetacean calves. A humpback whale calf, a three-week-old dolphin, and a melon-head whale calf were all seen in the test area. "We have never observed or heard of anyone observing an abandoned calf in our nine years of research off the Hawai'ian Islands," says OMI's Marsha Green. "That these abandoned calves appeared only in the test area and nowhere else suggests . . . further investigation. The sonar tests may cause disorientation so the mother and calf become separated and then cannot find each other."

During this phase a diver off Kona, unaware of the test, became disoriented and nauseated upon exposure to a 120dB source. A physician diagnosed symptoms comparable to acute trauma. Human divers have been hospitalized and treated for seizures and longer-term health effects after exposure to LFA sonar.

Questioning the Results

While the details of the LFA studies [were] revealed with the release of an Environmental Impact Assessment [in 1999], fundamental problems with the tests remain. The equipment the Navy intends to deploy has not been declassified; civilian scientists and public entities cannot study it. Further, short-term observations of whale behavior are not the best indication of how exposure might affect whales. Humpback whales exposed to high dB explosions and drilling off Newfoundland in 1993 revealed only small changes in residency, movements and general behavior. Three days later, two of those humpbacks died after becoming entangled in fishing nets, and subsequent necropsies revealed severe auditory damage. Important physiological systems and decisions are based on a whale's ability to detect and interpret sound at very faint levels.

LFA field studies were conducted using omni-directional sound pulses at roughly 150dB. The actual LFA sonar would use focused sound at 240dB, perhaps reaching 270dB; the beams' efficiency greatly increases from being focused and would travel up to 100 miles. As 240dB is approximately 100,000 times louder than the tests' 150db levels, the EIA does little to indicate LFA's impact.

Some critics feel the EIA is being carried out by researchers under contract to tell the Navy, one of the few remaining funding powerhouses for marine research, what it wants to hear; that "the loudest noises ever generated by man will not adversely affect whales and dolphins." The Navy seems confident in these conclusions and has no plans to halt deployment of LFA, barring effective public protest or litigation by a growing coalition of marine and environmental groups.

"*The potential impact [of Low Frequency Active sonar] on any one marine mammal from significant change in a biologically important behavior . . . is considered minimal.*"

Antisubmarine Sonar Does Not Threaten Marine Mammals

Dennis V. McGinn

The Surveillance Towed Array Sonar System, Low Frequency Active (LFA) is necessary to protect national security and has a minimal impact on marine mammals, argues Vice-Admiral Dennis V. McGinn, deputy chief of Naval Operations for Warfare Requirements and Programs, in the following viewpoint. LFA sonar is necessary to protect national security, McGinn asserts, because traditional sonar cannot detect the new, quieter submarines that some hostile nations are developing. Tests to determine the impact of LFA sonar on marine mammals, he claims, showed only negligible changes in behavior. Moreover, he maintains, the U.S. Navy has implemented restrictions on frequency levels and installed equipment to monitor marine mammals in areas where LFA is used.

As you read, consider the following questions:
1. According to McGinn, why are submarines ideal weapons for some countries?
2. In the author's opinion, how did migrating gray whales react to LFA when used directly in their path?

Dennis V. McGinn, statement before the Subcommittee on Fisheries Conservation, Wildlife, and Oceans, Committee on Resources, U.S. House of Representatives, Washington, DC, October 11, 2001.

The Navy has an immediate, critical need for SURTASS LFA [Surveillance Towed Array Sensor System Low Frequency Active][1]. By law, the Navy's primary mission is to maintain, train and equip combat-ready Naval forces capable of winning wars, deterring aggression and maintaining freedom of the seas. Antisubmarine warfare, or ASW, is a critical part of that mission. The Chief of Naval Operations (CNO) has stated that ASW is essential to sea control and maritime dominance. Many nations throughout the world can employ submarines to deny access to forward regions or to significantly delay the execution of crucial Navy operations. Because of its inherent stealth, lethality, and affordability, the submarine is a powerful threat. In 1998 the Chief of Naval Operations emphasized the importance of ASW in protecting our national security and set the direction for achieving operational primacy in ASW. He stated that the Navy's goal is to have the best-trained ASW force in the world, with the right set of tools to prevail in any type of conflict. . . . My goal here today is to show you why I believe one of the primary ASW tools must be SURTASS LFA.

Defending Against Quiet Submarines

Many of the opponents of SURTASS LFA say that the Cold War is over and question the need for the SURTASS LFA system. Despite the end of the Cold War, the submarine threat remains real and in some ways has become more challenging. Of the approximately 500 non-U.S. submarines in the world, 224 are operated by non-allied nations. Many of these are the more advanced, quieter diesel-electric submarines that present a real threat to U.S. forces. The Russian Federation and the People's Republic of China have publicly declared that the submarine is the capital ship of their navies. Many potential adversarial countries have es-

1. On July 16, 2002, the U.S. Department of Defense authorized the U.S. Navy to employ the Surveillance Towed Array Sonar System, Low Frequency Active (LFA) under restrictions it believed would reduce adverse effects on the marine environment. On October 31, 2002, the U.S. District Court for the Northern District of California granted a preliminary injunction, ordering the Navy to cease employing LFA sonar. The court set a hearing for June 2003, during which the parties will have agreed on how LFA sonar can be used so that the impact on marine mammals is limited.

sentially done the same, including Iran and North Korea. A former Indian Navy submarine admiral has commented that developing nations desire submarine forces because they are the most cost-effective platform for the delivery of several types of weapons; they counter surface forces effectively; they are flexible, multi-mission ships; they are covert and can operate with minimal political ramifications; and they can operate without supporting escorts. Submarines are ideal weapons for states that lack, or cannot afford, the capability to assert sea control in their own (or others') waterspace. They can operate in an opponent's backyard. Even in the face of determined sea control efforts, they can conduct stealthy and intrusive operations in sensitive areas, and can be inserted early for a wide range of tasks with a high degree of assured survivability. When equipped with mines, advanced torpedoes, anti-ship or land-attack missiles, a submarine is a potent tactical and political weapon. . . . In today's unpredictable world, we must recognize that the advanced, quiet submarine is potentially a terrorist threat. A single diesel-electric submarine that is able to penetrate U.S. or multinational task force's defenses could easily undermine military efforts to thwart hostile enemy forces and change the balance of political support for U.S. involvement in armed conflict. . . .

Quieting technology continues to proliferate, which will render these advanced diesel submarines difficult, if not nearly impossible to detect, even with the latest passive sonar equipment. This is where SURTASS LFA comes in—its state-of-the-art towed array provides the Navy with the world's best deep and shallow-water (littoral zone) low frequency passive acoustic sensor, called SURTASS. When SURTASS by itself proves inadequate in detecting and tracking submarines, its active component, LFA, is used—which is a set of acoustic transmitting source elements suspended by cable beneath the ship. These elements, called projectors, produce the active sound pulse, or "ping," which allows for such long-range detections of otherwise concealed submarines. Its extended detection ranges are achieved using low-frequency signals in the 100–500 Hertz frequency band, and high-gain receivers in the SURTASS towed array to pick up the returning echoes from the ping reflecting off the target submarine. Thus, SURTASS LFA meets the U.S. need for improved capability to detect quieter and hard-to-find foreign submarines at long range, and provides adequate time to react to and defend against potential submarine threats. . . .

The Environmental Impact Statement

The SURTASS LFA, EIS [Environmental Impact Statement] is the most comprehensive and exhaustive scientifically-based EIS ever undertaken by the Navy for a major seagoing combat system. Moreover, the Navy has gone to virtually unprecedented lengths to inform and involve the public. Since the release of the Notice of Intent in the Federal Register five years ago, the Navy has held three public scoping meetings in 1996, eight public outreach meetings in 1997–98, and three public hearings on the Draft EIS in 1999. Written and oral comments on the Draft EIS were received from over 1,000 commentors, including federal, state, regional and local agencies, environmental groups and associations, as well as private individuals. In addition, the Navy established the SURTASS LFA Scientific Working Group (SWG) in 1997. This distinguished panel was made up of independent scientists from a wide variety of marine laboratory and academic organizations, as well as a representative from the nongovernmental environmental groups opposed to LFA. The panel met periodically to determine the critical data gaps that needed to be addressed to evaluate the effects of low frequency sound on the marine environment, and to review the results from the SRP [Scientific Research Program] field experiments. . . .

Phase I was conducted with blue and fin whales feeding off the southern California coast, using three research vessels, including the *Cory Chouest* with the LFA system on it, small aircraft for aerial surveys, autonomous seafloor acoustic recording units, and the Navy's sound surveillance system, or SOSUS. This was the most extensive real-world field experiment using large baleen whales that has ever been undertaken. Initial analysis of SRP Phase I data indicated a slight decrease in whale vocal activity during LFA transmissions. However, subsequent, more detailed analysis using data from all three types of passive receivers on ships

185

and the seafloor showed no significant differences in vocal activity between the LFA transmission periods and the non-transmission periods.

Phase II was conducted with gray whales migrating southward along the central California coast, using a boat with a single LFA source element deployed over-the-side, an observation boat with hydrophones deployed over-the-side to verify received levels at the whales, and shore observers using state-of-the-art theodolite telescopes to track the whales. Phase II was conducted by some of the same scientists who conducted similar testing in 1983 and 1984, which showed the gray whales reacting to 120 dB [decibel] received levels. During Phase II, when the sound source was placed directly in the path of the migrating gray whales, they showed a modest avoidance reaction by deflecting a few hundred yards around the source at received levels of 138 to 144 dB. However, when the source was moved one nautical mile farther out to sea and the source level adjusted so that the exposure level at the animals in the migration corridor remained the same, the whales did not exhibit avoidance of the signal.

Studying Whale Interactions

Phase III was conducted with breeding humpback whales off the Kona coast of the Big Island of Hawaii, using *Cory Chouest* with the LFA system, a Navy SURTASS ship with its passive towed array, an observation boat to verify received levels at the whales, and shore observers with theodolite telescopes. During Phase III, about half of the singing humpback whales showed what at first appeared to be avoidance level responses and cessation of singing when exposed to LFA signals at received levels of 120–155 dB. However, an equal number of singing whales exposed to the same levels of LFA signals showed no avoidance or cessation of song. Of the whales that did stop singing, there was little response to subsequent LFA transmissions, as most joined with other whales or resumed singing within less than an hour of exposure to the LFA sounds. Those that did not stop singing, sang longer songs during LFA transmissions, and returned to their baseline levels after LFA transmissions stopped. The independent scientists who designed and conducted this experiment determined that this brief interruption, followed by resumption of normal interactions, is similar to that seen when whales interrupt one another or when small vessels, like whale-watching boats, approach an animal. If whales are in a breeding habitat and such vessel interactions are frequent, the aggregate impact of all disruptive stimuli could effect significant biological functions. However, LFA will be operated well offshore of humpback breeding areas. It is highly likely that the cumulative impact of numerous inshore vessel interactions will cause significantly greater impact on these animals than that caused by infrequent offshore LFA transmissions.

How Navy SURTASS LFA Vessels Will Monitor Marine Mammals

- Visual monitoring for marine mammals and sea turtles from the SURTASS LFA sonar vessel during daylight hours;
- Passive (low frequency) SURTASS array to listen for sounds generated by marine mammals as an indicator of their presence; and
- High frequency (HF) active sonar to detect/locate/track potentially affected marine mammals (and possibly sea turtles) near the SURTASS LFA sonar vessel and the sound field produced by the SURTASS LFA sonar source array.

U.S. Department of the Navy, Surtass-lfa-eis.com, 2002.

In summary, this $10 million SRP, conducted independently by world-renowned marine biologists and bioacousticians, collected much-needed data on the reaction of marine mammals considered to be most susceptible to low frequency sounds—baleen whales. The results of these field studies led to the determination that the LFA sonar system could be operated safely with the restrictions and mitigation proposed in the EIS. . . .

Mitigating the Effects

Extensive mitigation and monitoring requirements will be levied on all LFA operations. Geographic restrictions dictate that received levels will always be below 180 dB within 12 nautical miles of any coastline, and any NOAA [National Oceanic and Atmospheric Administration] and Navy-designated offshore biologically important area. Received levels will not exceed 145 dB in the vicinity of any known commercial or recreational dive sites. Monitoring mitigation procedures include daylight visual monitoring for marine mammals and sea turtles, passive listening with the SUR-TASS towed array to detect sounds generated by marine mammals as an indicator of their presence, and high frequency sonar to detect, locate and track marine mammals, and possibly sea turtles, near the LFA vessel to ensure they do not enter the 180-dB LFA Mitigation Zone.

The SRP field study results demonstrate that, while not impossible, the planned operations of LFA are highly unlikely to cause injury, especially given the operational restrictions and mitigation measures that will be employed in conjunction with all LFA operations. Extensive analysis has shown that a small number of animals will be exposed to levels above 165 dB, up to a maximum range from the source of approximately 30 nautical miles under optimal acoustic propagation conditions that may occur no more than 10 percent of the time. In general, exposure levels are more dependent on the depth of the animal than its range from the source. Therefore, the 30-nautical mile maximum needs to be tempered with the depth dependence of the sound field. Received levels up to 140 dB can range out to 300 nautical miles but, again, only under optimal conditions and assuming the animal is located in the narrow depth zone of highest sound level. At these ranges, the animal will move out of the small volume of high sound energy by simply changing depth. In ocean areas with water depths less than 4,000 feet, the ranges are significantly shorter (down to 10 percent of the above maximum ranges).

It is possible to *hear* LFA at long ranges. However, merely *hearing* the LFA signal does not constitute an impact—an important point that LFA opponents fail to acknowledge time and again. Given that the LFA signal does not seem to be intrinsically threatening or annoying to marine mammals, in the case of simply being able to hear the signal, the animal will necessarily be far from the source. Thus, it will not find itself within the area where a significant change to a biologically important behavior could occur; more than likely animals will have no reaction at these low exposure levels.

In summary, the potential impact on any stock of marine mammals from injury is considered negligible. The potential impact on any one marine mammal from significant change in a biologically important behavior—such as migrating, breeding, feeding, or sheltering—is considered minimal.

"The public display of marine mammals plays an integral role in [the] conservation effort, helping to preserve these magnificent animals for present and future generations."

Keeping Marine Mammals Captive in Theme Parks Promotes Conservation

George Mannina

The public display of marine mammals plays an important role in promoting the conservation of these creatures, argues environmental lawyer George Mannina in the following viewpoint, originally given as testimony before a House Subcommittee. Mannina contends that organizations such as the American Zoo and Aquarium Association and the Alliance of Marine Mammal Parks and Aquariums have established marine park educational programs that have raised visitors' awareness of the need to protect marine mammals. Moreover, marine parks conduct research that adds to scientists' understanding of marine mammals and provide refuge for injured or stranded wild marine mammals.

As you read, consider the following questions:

1. What improvements and advancements have resulted from marine park studies of marine mammals, in Mannina's view?
2. What success stories does the author cite to demonstrate the role marine parks play in the rescue and rehabilitation of marine mammals?

George Mannina, testimony before the Subcommittee on Fisheries Conservation, Wildlife, and Oceans, Committee on Resources, U.S. House of Representatives, Washington, DC, October 11, 2001.

M r. Chairman and Members of the Subcommittee, I am representing the American Zoo and Aquarium Association (AZA) and the Alliance of Marine Mammal Parks and Aquariums (Alliance). The members of these two organizations include marine life parks, aquariums, and zoos whose expertise is the public display of animals including marine mammals. These zoological institutions are dedicated to the highest standards of care for marine mammals and to their conservation in the wild through public education, scientific study, and wildlife presentations. Collectively, the members of AZA and the Alliance represent the greatest body of experience and knowledge with respect to marine mammal husbandry.

The Role of Public Display Facilities

AZA represents over 200 accredited zoo and aquarium institutions that draw over 135 million visitors annually and have more than 5 million zoo and aquarium members. The Alliance has 40 members that host over 36 million visitors each year. Collectively, these institutions teach more than 12 million people each year in living classrooms, dedicate over $50 million annually to education programs, invest over $50 million annually to scientific research and support over 1300 field conservation and research projects in 80 countries.

AZA and the Alliance are uniquely qualified to comment on the Marine Mammal Protection Act (MMPA). Both organizations are very knowledgeable about the MMPA as it pertains to the public display of marine mammals and the rescue of stranded animals. And, both were actively involved in the process of amending the MMPA in 1994.

The House Resources Committee and its Subcommittee on Fisheries Conservation, Wildlife and Oceans have long understood the important role of public display. Indeed, a Congressional report on the passage of Marine Mammal Protection Act in 1972 observed ". . . without observing marine mammals in oceanaria the 'magnificent interest' in marine mammals will be lost and 'none will ever see them and none will care about them and they will be extinct. If it were not for these organizations and the public exposure you have on these animals in the first place, these matters wouldn't be brought to the attention of the public.'"

The Value of Education

The conservation of marine mammals requires public education, the practice of conservation behaviors by every individual, and the development of effective public policy. The public display of marine mammals plays an integral role in this conservation effort, helping to preserve these magnificent animals for present and future generations. With public display comes marine mammal education and conservation programs unique in their ability to establish a personal connection between visitors and the animals. This personal connection fosters learning about how the behaviors of each and every one of us affect marine mammals and the habitats in which they dwell.

Congress has entrusted zoological parks and aquariums with great responsibility and they strive daily to live up to that responsibility. Each and every year, members of the American Zoo and Aquarium Association and the Alliance of Marine Mammal Parks and Aquariums proudly communicate their educational messages to an ever-expanding and diverse audience, reaching more and more children and adults about the importance of conserving marine mammals and their habitats. Members provide an enthusiastic, imaginative, and intellectually stimulating environment to the approximately 140 million people who visit AZA and Alliance member marine life parks, aquariums, and zoos annually. Additionally, each year over 12 million young people participate in programs for school children. With the growth of the Internet, along with more traditional forms of communication, AZA and Alliance members reach nearly one hundred and fifty million children and adults each year.

Recognizing this responsibility, both AZA and the Alliance established standards for education programs offered by public display facilities in the United States. The standards have been acknowledged by the National Marine Fisheries Service (NMFS) as the two "professionally accepted standards" on which a public display facility must base its education and conservation programs. NMFS published these standards in the *Federal Register* October 6, 1994, (Vol. 59, No. 193, Pgs. 50900–2).

The mission of educational exhibits and programming at

AZA and Alliance member facilities is to enhance the appreciation and understanding of marine mammals and their ecosystems. Members of these zoological institutions instill in those who visit an awareness of ecological and conservation issues and a respect and caring for these animals and their environments. Our members believe this respect engenders a strong, active commitment to marine mammal conservation and an understanding that each and every person can make a difference. . . .

Teaching the Importance of Conservation

A 1998 Roper Starch poll provides clear evidence that programs at marine life parks, aquariums, and zoos are educational and provide the public with a heightened appreciation of the importance of conserving and preserving marine mammals. Responses to the Roper Starch poll indicate that seeing live marine mammals enhances the educational experience for the visitors to marine life parks, aquariums, and zoos.

- Almost everyone (97%) who visited Alliance member marine life parks, aquariums, and zoos said their experience with live marine mammals had an impact on their appreciation and knowledge of the animals. The impact was greater for those visiting facilities where they actually had an opportunity to interact with marine mammals.
- Ninety-six percent (96%) of the parks' visitors agreed that "seeing marine mammals engaged in their daily behavior as I did here today is the best way to understand and learn about them."
- Ninety-four percent (94%) of the visitors agreed with the statement, "I learned a great deal about marine mammals today."
- Nine in ten visitors agreed that they "have become more concerned about the importance of preservation/ conservation of marine mammals as a result of my visit here today."

The Need for Research

Knowledge acquired through research with animals in public display facilities, in tandem with field research, is another fundamental contribution to marine mammal conservation.

Communicating this knowledge is one of the most effective means of ensuring the health of wild marine mammals in the 21st century. Much of this research simply cannot be accomplished in ocean conditions.

Education Program Standards of the Alliance of Marine Mammal Parks and Aquariums

1. Education programs about marine mammals must promote an improved understanding of and an appreciation for these animals and their ecosystems.

2. Education programs about marine mammals must offer multiple levels of learning opportunities for visitors to expand their knowledge about these animals.

3. Education programs about marine mammals must present information about these animals, their ecosystem, or marine wildlife conservation that is based upon the best current scientific knowledge.

4. A qualified individual must be designated and responsible for the development of, and administration of, education programs about marine mammals.

5. Education programs about marine mammals must include a written education plan consisting of a mission statement, goals, and an evaluation strategy.

6. Education programs about marine mammals must include availability of institution experts as a marine science resource to professional groups and the education community when appropriate and practicable.

National Marine Fisheries Service, *Federal Register*, October 6, 1994.

Tens of millions of dollars are being spent on research at and by AZA and Alliance member facilities that is essential in understanding the anatomy and physiology of marine mammals, in treating sick and injured animals from the wild, and in learning to better manage and assist endangered species. Additionally, many AZA and Alliance facilities collaborate with marine mammal researchers from colleges, universities, and other scientific institutions that conduct studies important to wild species' conservation and health. Over the years, this body of work has contributed significantly to the present knowledge about marine mammal biology, physiology, reproduction, behavior and conservation.

These studies have led to improvements in diagnosing and treating diseases; techniques for anesthesia and surgery; tests for toxic substances and their effects on wild marine mammals; and advancements in diet, vitamin supplementation, and neonatal feeding.

There is still a tremendous amount scientists do not yet know about the marine mammals in our oceans and rivers. And we desperately need greater knowledge and understanding if we are going to make informed, intelligent decisions regarding the increasingly complex pressures on these wild animals. The long-term studies of in-shore, wild marine mammal populations, which provide scientists opportunities to measure contaminant exposure, monitor health and immune responses of individual animals, and to study population-level trends, are extremely important. . . .

Recovering Stranded Marine Mammals

For centuries, experts have long been frustrated in their attempt to restore to health the millions of stranded marine mammals found sick and dying on beaches throughout the world. Today, members of AZA and the Alliance have the expertise and ability to offer much needed, practical assistance to these animals. The accumulated knowledge, collective experience, and resources of these facilities are the primary factors in these successful rehabilitation efforts. Indeed, AZA and Alliance members provide millions of dollars in direct expenditures and in-kind contributions annually to support stranding programs.

Though there are hundreds of unspoken heroes who strive to save stranded marine mammals, one recent event was highlighted in a documentary by National Public Television. It featured Mystic Aquarium's successful rehabilitation of a pair of young pilot whales. The show was titled *Whale Rescue: Stranded Friends*. The pair of whales were rescued from a Cape Cod beach and, after being nursed back to health for nearly four months, were released off the coast of Rhode Island. It was the first release of pilot whales by any U.S. aquarium in nearly 14 years. The whales were fitted with satellite-linked transmitters that operated for approximately three months and provided aquarium scientists with important information about the animals' range and diving patterns.

Also, Animal Planet's *Wild Rescues* featured a segment on Dually, an injured manatee rescued in the Florida Keys. The show contains dramatic footage of Dually's initial rescue by the Dolphin Research Center and her surgery at Miami Seaquarium to remove fishing line embedded in her flippers.

The U.S. Coast Guard flew a melon-headed whale calf to Sea Life Park Hawaii after it was found floundering in the ocean two years ago. These whales are not found in public display facilities and scientists from the University of Hawaii are using this unique opportunity to learn more about the species and its acoustic behavior.

Mass strandings are becoming more common. Over 100 dolphins died in bays along the Florida panhandle in late 1999 and early 2000. Another 100 dolphins stranded and 28 died . . . in the Florida Keys. AZA and Alliance members located throughout Florida cooperated with government officials in efforts to save the animals involved in the mass strandings in their state waters. . . .

Both AZA and the Alliance very much appreciate the opportunity to testify before the Subcommittee today and hope our comments have been helpful.

"Captivity severely compromises a whale or dolphin's quality of life. In the wild, they have complex social lives which cannot be recreated in captivity."

Keeping Marine Mammals Captive in Theme Parks Is Cruel

Whale and Dolphin Conservation Society

In the following viewpoint the Whale and Dolphin Conservation Society (WDCS) argues that keeping marine mammals captive in marine theme parks is cruel. Whales and dolphins that normally swim in open oceans do not live as long when confined in captivity, WDCS claims, and some become injured when the stress of captivity leads to aggressive behavior. Forcing dolphins to swim with humans is particularly cruel and dangerous, WDCS maintains, because captive dolphins—who have nowhere to hide—may bite when they no longer want to interact with humans. The argument that captive mammals provide research and educational opportunities is unfounded because captive behavior is not the same as behavior in the wild, WDCS asserts.

As you read, consider the following questions:

1. According to WDCS, why do marine parks want successful marine mammal breeding programs?
2. What has WDCS witnessed in America's dolphin petting pools?
3. How does the WDCS view Dolphin Assisted Therapy programs?

Captivity severely compromises a whale or dolphin's quality of life. In the wild, they have complex social lives which cannot be recreated in captivity.

Why Keeping Whales and Dolphins Is Cruel

Dolphins have been kept in terrible conditions; for such a graceful, wide-ranging animal no holding pools can be adequate. Similarly, no-one should be fooled by the attractive backdrops which some dolphinariums add to their pools. This is purely for our benefit not the dolphins.

Bottlenose dolphins are particularly famed for their friendly faces; however this can mask depression, stress and frustration. There are numerous cases of whales and dolphins displaying aggression towards humans and other dolphins in captivity. During aggression between dolphins there is nowhere to escape to; as a result struggles often end with injuries. This is rarely seen in the wild.

Current conservation philosophies around the world focus on saving natural habitats: removing dolphins from the wild is contrary to this philosophy.

The survival rate of captive-born whale and dolphin calves is lower than those in the wild. Any arguments presented by marine parks that they are involved in breeding programmes are without foundation. Their primary reason for achieving a successful breeding programme is to maintain a supply of performing animals, as regulations gradually make it more difficult to capture wild dolphins.

Aside from all these reasons, WDCS [the Whale and Dolphin Conservation Society] considers it immoral and unethical to imprison these wonderful creatures. This stance is increasingly being reflected in public opinion; for example, in the UK [United Kingdom] the findings of a 1996 MORI Poll demonstrated that 85% of those surveyed thought it 'unacceptable' to keep whales and dolphins in captivity. The main reasons quoted were: 'it's not natural' and 'they should be swimming freely in the sea'.

It is almost impossible to track accurately the movements of captive dolphins from facility to facility. Some dolphins travel miles in their performing life; for example, "Sheryl", a Black Sea bottlenose dolphin, was held in Russia and then transported to Argentina in 1991. She ended up in a South American travelling circus and finally died in Colombia in 1997. Dolphins captured in Cuba have ended up in the Caribbean, Germany, Spain, Italy, Switzerland and many other countries across Europe, South America and Asia.

The Expansion of the "Dolphin Show"

The United States, Canada, Central and South America, Asia, the Middle East and some European countries continue to actively promote dolphin shows. However, it is the US that has been particularly effective in finding new ways to develop the show to increase revenue and encouraged other countries to follow suit. Nowadays, when you visit a dolphinarium, you pay to see the show, pay to pet the dolphins, pay to feed the dolphins or even pay to swim with them. Once you have experienced all of that, there is a club to join and numerous souvenirs and toys to buy. Suddenly, you will have been parted from all your money, without even realising it!

Petting Pools usually comprise a group of dolphins competing to be fed small dead fish by tourists. All of the SeaWorld parks in America now have these 'attractions'. The popularity of Petting Pools as another way of extracting money from the excited tourist is particularly concerning for a number of reasons. WDCS has witnessed: over-fed, fat dolphins in these pools; dolphins biting people in their attempt to get the fish; tourists cruelly teasing dolphins, and people dropping inappropriate objects into the pool, such as sunglasses and beer.

Furthermore, some of the fish fed to the dolphins may become contaminated through man-handling and falling to the floor and it is also difficult to regulate the amount of food fed to the dolphins. The petting pool concept sends conflicting messages to the visiting public, as zoos normally strictly prohibit the feeding of animals.

Swimming with Dolphins

Many people have a desire to 'swim with' dolphins. This is providing dolphinariums with yet another way of increasing revenue. Again, as it is cruel to keep dolphins to perform, it is cruel to enforce interactions with humans day after day. There is also a concern that there may be disease transmission between dolphin and human, plus the danger of potential aggressive behaviour, which has been documented.

The Facts About Swim-with-Dolphins Facilities

The fact that these facilities love their dolphins is not the point. No one questions their love for the animals. After all, who doesn't love dolphins? That's why so many people are willing to spend hundreds of dollars to participate in these programs. The real issue is whether swim-with programs have the dolphin's best interest at heart. Remember, these are for-profit businesses that thrive by keeping their expenses low and working the dolphins as much as possible. Do you really believe that a dolphin is happier having people ride around on its back and eating dead fish than it would be frolicking freely with other dolphins in its natural environment?

The truth, whether it's called behavior training or positive reinforcement, is that dolphins perform tricks in front of cheering spectators because they are hungry. It's that simple. Whether food is used to positively reward correct behavior such as a successful back flip or withheld to punish incorrect behavior like ignoring a trainer's command, it still amounts to food deprivation. Dolphin trainers know that if a dolphin has a stomach full of fish, it won't perform. Call it what you will—performing dolphins are the victims of selective starvation. Does this seem like a loving way to treat dolphins?

World Society for the Protection of Animals, "Fact Versus Ficion," www. freethedolphins.org, February 4, 2003.

Dolphin interaction programmes, from touching and feeding to swimming with dolphins are increasing in range and popularity. Love for dolphins may encourage members of the public to want to get close to them. This desire may stem from the belief that close contact with these special animals can provide, at the very least, a spiritual release from day to day stresses and boredom and at the other extreme some sort of miracle cure for disease and mental illness. Such beliefs have helped encourage the growth of interaction programmes by both commercial interests and alternative therapists.

WDCS is increasingly concerned about the growing number of so-called Dolphin Assisted Therapy (DAT) programmes in the United States, Latin America and elsewhere. We are currently reviewing details of existing and proposed DAT programmes and investigating whether "benefits" claimed by or on behalf of patients using this kind of therapy are equivalent to those claimed in less controversial interactions with puppies, horses and other domesticated animals. We would be interested to hear your views, and perhaps your personal experiences with all kinds of animal assisted therapy. Please write to us.

The Consequences for Humans and Dolphins

WDCS has a series of well-substantiated concerns about interactions between humans and dolphins in captivity and, indeed, in the wild. These concerns, relating to the welfare of humans as well as dolphins, apply equally to dolphin assisted therapy. They include the welfare of the animal; the risk of aggression towards people; the potential for disease transmission from human to dolphin or vice versa; the fact that dolphins may be forced into interactions with humans and have little refuge or respite from these actions and the fact that in so many DAT and other interaction programmes, dolphins are captured from the wild and/or transported thousands of miles to suffer the effects of confinement in captivity.

Dolphins are large, strong animals perfectly adapted to the conditions of the open ocean. Held in a confined space and subjected to forced interaction with humans, aggressive behaviour can have serious consequences. A recent study carried out by WDCS into dolphin/visitor interactions at marine parks in America records many incidents of aggressive behaviour by dolphins towards human visitors such as threats, biting and butting. This study also raises serious concerns regarding the potential for the transmission of disease between human visitors and dolphins.

Inadequate regulations exist in relation to interactions between captive dolphins and members of the public. WDCS is bringing its concerns and evidence to the attention of relevant governments and other interested parties, who must address the potential consequences for both humans and dolphins of these interaction programmes.

The "Scientific Research" Justification

Marine parks continue to argue that they play an important part in marine mammal research. This is one of the widely-used justifications for captivity. Parks claim to provide the general public and science with useful knowledge. However, a WDCS review of scientific research in dolphinariums throws serious doubt on these claims, as this research has little relevance to the conservation of free-living whales and dolphins.

The debatable value of captive research can be easily demonstrated. There are many papers published on training techniques which have no relevance to conservation. Disease studies on captive dolphins have identified what diseases and parasitic burdens are present. However, this knowledge cannot be applied usefully in the wild, as captive dolphins live in an artificial environment and are fed with various drugs, which alter their body chemistry. Knowledge from captive studies of disease has also contributed nothing to preventing or predicting the recent outbreaks of viruses in wild dolphin populations, which can cause mass mortalities.

Basic reproductive information on pregnancies and sexual maturity has been obtained for some species in captivity. It would be dangerous to apply this information directly to the conservation and management of wild populations as it may over-estimate their reproductive capacities. Feeding has a marked effect on these areas and the unnatural composition of zoo diets means that their natural growth patterns may be different. Studies conducted on whale and dolphin behaviour in captivity do not have the potential to improve the conservation of wild cetaceans, as captive animals' lives are artificial. They follow the same basic routine rather than the varied daily movements of a free-living cetacean.

For these reasons, WDCS does not consider captive research valid to the conservation of whales and dolphins in the wild.

Many dolphinariums claim that they are playing an important role in educating people to appreciate the marine environment, and in fact, some regulatory bodies require dolphinariums to demonstrate an 'educational value' to their displays. WDCS believes that marine parks significantly distort the public's understanding of the marine environment. Educational messages take second place to the whale and dolphin performances, where the "jumping" and "splashing" are the main feature. Any educational aspects are lost amidst the glamour and excitement. Similarly, the complex nature of the lives of whales and dolphins cannot possibly be demonstrated in a tank.

Some marine parks also distort the real truth behind captivity by using different words. For example, whales and dolphins are 'acquired' rather than 'captured'; captives do not live in tanks, they live in 'controlled environments'. Such terminology only serves to distract the visitor's eye from the reality of tanks and repetitive daily routines.

It is easier now than it ever has been to see whales and dolphins in the wild. This experience cannot be improved upon for excitement and education. Imagine going out on a trip as a child. You will learn about whales and dolphins in their natural habitat and you will see their natural behaviour. You will also learn about the boat, about the ocean and the other creatures which live in it. The experience will teach you that, as a human, you cannot and should not control or tame everything: an important lesson in conservation. . . .

Criticism and Counterarguments

"Our animals are happy". . . Dolphins have a natural smile on their face, they also die smiling.

"The seas are polluted and dangerous, here they are protected". . . Whales and dolphins have evolved over millions of years to live in the ocean, it is their natural habitat. The way to solve pollution and other environmental problems is to tackle the point sources of pollution, not take species out of the seas.

"Why are people campaigning against captivity when there are other more endangered species that need protecting?". . . WDCS funds cetacean research and conservation on many endangered species. WDCS also protects the individual cetacean as well as cetaceans in the wild. The captivity campaign is just one small facet of the work we do.

"Whales and dolphins in captivity have forgotten how to live in the wild". . . Dolphins have been successfully released into the wild. Whales and dolphins are intelligent creatures, if they can learn tricks that aren't necessary for survival then they can learn how to be wild again.

Periodical Bibliography

The following articles have been selected to supplement the diverse views presented in this chapter.

William Aron, William Burke, and Milton Freeman	"Scientists Versus Whaling: Science, Advocacy, and Errors of Judgment," *Bioscience*, December 2002.
Stan Butler	"Pandora's Whale: A Tribal Whale Hunt May Open a Floodgate of Commercial Whaling," *Christian Science Monitor*, October 15, 1998.
Leigh Calvez	"Deafness in the Depths," *Ecologist*, June 2000.
Michael De Alessi and Robert J. Smith	"A Whale of a Tale: The Promise of Private Conservation for Whales," *Stewardship Chronicles*, August 2, 2001.
Phil Fontana and Chip Gill	"Marine Mammals and Seismic Vessels Jockey for Position," *World Oil*, December 2002.
Greenpeace	"Dying for a Ban: Japan and Norway Continue to Slaughter Whales," *Greenpeace Magazine*, Summer 1998.
Peter Hadfield	"A Very Fishy Tale: How Japan Defends Whaling Research," *New Scientist*, October 21, 2000.
Sidney Hold	"To Whale or Not to Whale," *Ecologist*, February 2002.
James Hrynyshyn	"Going Round the Bend: Noise Can Bring on Decompression Sickness in Whales and Dolphins," *New Scientist*, December 15, 2001.
David Malakoff	"A Roaring Debate over Ocean Noise," *Science*, January 26, 2001.
Amy Mathews-Amos and Ewann A. Bernston	"Climate Change Harms Ocean Life," *Earth Island Journal*, Fall 1999.
James B. McGirk	"The Whaling Commission Flounders," *Foreign Policy*, September/October 2002.
Mark J. Palmer	"Keep the 'Dolphin Safe' Tuna Label Honest," *Earth Island Journal*, Summer 1999.
Joni Praded	"The Trouble with Dolphin Swims: Why Swim-with-Dolphin Programs Have Some Folks Making Waves," *Animals*, Winter 2002.
Margi Prideaux	"Whale Wars," *Habitat Australia*, February 2000.

Margi Prideaux and Mike Bossley	"Lethal Waters: The Assault on Our Marine Mammals," *Habitat Australia*, April 2000.
Michael A. Rivlin	"Northern Exposure," *OnEarth*, Fall 2001.
Dick Russell	"The Whale Killers," *E Magazine*, January/ February 2003.
Wendy Williams	"Not-So-Silent Seas," *Audubon*, September 2002.

For Further Discussion

Chapter 1

1. Anne Platt McGinn claims that attempts to manage the impact of human activities on the world's oceans and coastal areas have failed to protect the marine ecosystem. Frank E. Loy is more optimistic, citing the success of various marine conservation efforts. Do you share Loy's optimism, or do you agree with McGinn? Explain, citing evidence from both viewpoints.

2. Carl Safina believes that current fishery management strategies are ineffective in promoting sustainable fisheries. Do you think the private conservation strategies recommended by Michael De Alessi would be sufficient to effect the kinds of changes that Safina believes are necessary to promote sustainable fisheries? Why or why not?

3. Don Hinrichsen assumes the accuracy of predictions made by the Intergovernmental Panel on Climate Change (IPCC) that sea levels are rising. Hinrichsen focuses his argument on the tremendous economic and social costs of rising sea levels. However, John L. Daly claims that IPCC predictions are based on a theoretical model that does not prove sea levels have risen or will rise in the future. If Daly is correct and a theoretical model can not actually prove rising sea levels, do you think the predictions should be dismissed, or should people still implement reforms to protect coastal populations from sea level rise? Why or why not?

Chapter 2

1. Ted Thompson argues that because the cruise ship industry has a vested interest, it can be counted on to protect the marine environment. Kira Schmidt, on the other hand, offers evidence that the cruise ship industry is not a good steward of the marine environment. Citing evidence from the texts, whose position do you find most persuasive?

2. The marine protected area (MPA) debate centers around what activities will be prohibited. Sherman Baynard, who represents recreational fishers, claims that before an MPA is established, its purpose should be specifically and scientifically defined. The National Oceanic and Atmospheric Administration lists several activities that may be prohibited in MPAs. Select one of these activities and examine how individuals, businesses, or organizations with an interest in this activity might want to restrict how MPAs are defined.

3. Michael Markels and Richard T. Barber claim that ocean fertilization is the most efficient and economical solution to the problem of increased carbon dioxide levels in the atmosphere. Sallie W. Chisholm and her colleagues argue that the iron hypothesis is unproven and that ocean fertilization could adversely affect the marine ecology. Do you think Chisholm and her colleagues would approve of ocean fertilization if it were proven to solve the problem of CO_2 increases? What in the text led you to your conclusion?

Chapter 3

1. To increase depleted fish populations, David White recommends the widespread establishment of fully protected marine reserves that close ocean areas to fishing. White argues that while analysts debate whether these reserves are necessary, the risk to fish populations grows. Robert L. Shipp agrees that fully protected reserves are useful to increase the sustainability of some species, but argues that fully protected reserves can actually reduce the yield of other species and recommends a more cautious approach. Do you think the need to create fully protected marine reserves is urgent, or do you think more research is necessary before areas are completely closed to fishing? Explain, citing from the texts.

2. Once scientists determined the total allowable catch that would sustain ocean fisheries, fishers began to engage in a "race for the fish" within these limits. This race encouraged wasteful and dangerous fishing practices that further threatened fishing communities. Donald R. Leal claims that Individual Fishing Quotas (IFQs) will protect each fisher's allocation thus preventing the race for fish. However, Kaitilyn Gaffney maintains that allocations are not always fair and quotas do not always protect fish stocks. Who, in your view, provides the more convincing argument? Explain.

3. As a trade association, the National Aquaculture Association (NAA) has an economic stake in whether the aquaculture industry is forced to comply with additional (and undoubtedly costly) federal regulations. To support its position that existing regulation is already protecting wild fish stocks, the NAA explains that because aquaculture industries depend on the health of marine ecosystems, it is in their own best interest to protect them. Does this argument convince you that aquaculture producers will act voluntarily to minimize the risks that Rebecca J. Goldburg fears will damage the marine environment? Explain.

Chapter 4

1. Greenpeace claims that lifting the ban on commercial whaling in favor of managed whale hunting would lead to the same practices that devastated whale populations during the twentieth century. Greenpeace reasons that if whaling nations lie and cheat to increase their whale kills under the commercial whaling ban, they will likely do the same or worse under managed whaling schemes. How do William Aron, William Burke, and Milton Freeman answer these claims? Whose argument do you find more persuasive?

2. Nathan LaBudde and Dennis V. McGinn both refer to the U.S. Navy's environmental impact assessment of low-frequency sonar on whale populations to support their arguments. While LaBudde claims the whales' reactions to the sonar proves that the sonar can be harmful to marine mammals, McGinn maintains that these reactions demonstrate that the impact on marine mammals is minimal. What type of marine mammal behaviors do you think McGinn would consider harmful enough to forbid use of low-frequency sonar? What in the text of his viewpoint led you to your conclusion?

3. The Whale and Dolphin Conservation Society claims it is cruel to force marine mammals such as dolphins to interact with human beings. George Mannina, on the other hand, argues that when visitors are allowed to interact with marine mammals, their understanding for and appreciation of these animals increase. Do you think the educational value of these programs justifies forcing marine mammals to interact with human beings? Explain, citing from the texts.

Organizations to Contact

The editors have compiled the following list of organizations concerned with the issues debated in this book. The descriptions are derived from materials provided by the organizations. All have publications or information available for interested readers. The list was compiled on the date of publication of the present volume; the information provided here may change. Be aware that many organizations take several weeks or longer to respond to inquiries, so allow as much time as possible.

American Cetacean Society (ACS)
PO Box 1391, San Pedro, CA 90733
(310) 548-6279 • fax: (310) 548-6950
e-mail: info@acsonline.org • website: www.acsonline.org

A nonprofit volunteer membership organization, ACS works to protect whales, dolphins, porpoises, and their habitats through education, conservation, and research. The society aims to educate the public about cetaceans and the problems they face in their increasingly threatened habitats. Publications include fact sheets and reports as well as the society's research journal *Whalewatcher*, published twice a year. Recent publications and action alerts are available on the ACS website.

Coast Alliance
215 Pennsylvania Ave. SE, Washington, DC 20003
(202) 546-9554 • fax: (202) 546-9609
e-mail: coast@coastalliance.org • website: www.coastalliance.org

Coast Alliance is a nonprofit organization dedicated to protecting coastal resources and furthering public understanding of issues affecting the coastal areas of the nation. The alliance publishes numerous reports and a quarterly newsletter on the environment, conservation, and the effects of pollution, which are available on its website.

Greenpeace USA
702 H St. NW, Washington, DC 20001
(800) 326-0959 • fax: (202) 462-4507
e-mail: info@wdc.greenpeace.org • website:
www.greenpeaceusa.org

Greenpeace opposes nuclear energy and the use of toxic chemicals and supports ocean and wildlife preservation. It uses controversial direct-action techniques and strives for media coverage of its actions in an effort to educate the public. It publishes the quarterly magazine *Greenpeace* and the books *Coastline* and *The Greenpeace Book on Antarctica*. On its website Greenpeace publishes fact sheets and reports, including *Banning Factory Trawlers* and *Japanese Whaling: An Industry Out of Control*.

High North Alliance
PO Box 123, N-8390 Reine i Lofoten, Norway
(47) 76 09 24 14 • fax: (47) 76 09 24 50
e-mail: hna@highnorth.no • website: www.highnorth.no

The alliance is an umbrella organization that represents fishermen, whalers, and sealers from Canada, Greenland, Iceland, Norway, and various coastal communities. It is committed to the sustainable use of marine resources. Its publications include *Essays on Whales and Man* and the monthly newsletter *High North News*. On its website the alliance provides access to a library of fact sheets and reports.

Living Oceans Program
National Audubon Society
550 South Bay Ave., Islip, NY 11751
(516) 224-3669 • fax: (516) 581-5268
e-mail: livingoceans@audubon.org
website: http://audubon.org/campaign/lo

The Living Oceans Program is Audubon's marine conservation program. Its mission is to improve the management of fisheries, and to restore the health of the marine environment and coastal habitats by making scientifically based analyses and recommendations to policy makers and the public. The program publishes action alerts and the quarterly *Living Oceans News*, selections of which are available on its website.

National Fisheries Institute
1901 N. Fort Myer Dr., Suite 700, Arlington, VA 22209
(703) 524-8881 • fax: (703) 524-4619
e-mail: tressler@nfi.org • website: www.nfi.org

The institute is a nonprofit trade association representing more than 1,000 companies involved in all aspects of the fish and seafood industry. The institute acts to ensure an ample, sustainable, and safe seafood supply for consumers. It offers training and merchandising publications, fact sheets, and the monthly newsletter *NFI News*, which are available on its website.

Natural Resources Defense Council (NRDC)
40 West 20th St., New York, NY 10011
(212) 727-2700 • fax: (212) 727-1773
e-mail: nrdcinfo@nrdc.org • website: www.nrdc.org

The nonprofit NRDC, staffed by lawyers and scientists, conducts research and undertakes litigation on a broad range of environmental issues, including marine and coastal conservation. The council supports a strong federal role in environmental policy making. NRDC publishes reports such as *Keeping Oceans Wild: How Marine Reserves Protect Our Living Seas* and the quarterly *OnEarth* magazine. On its website NRDC provides access to reports on oceans, fish, and marine wildlife and excerpts from *OnEarth*.

Ocean Conservancy
1725 DeSales St. NW, Suite 600, Washington, DC 20036
(202) 429-5609 • fax: (202) 872-0619
e-mail: rrufe@oceanconservancy.org
website: www.oceanconservancy.org

Through science-based advocacy, research, and public education, the goal of the Ocean Conservancy is to inform, inspire, and empower people to speak and act for the oceans. The conservancy strives to conserve marine fish populations, restore clean coastal and ocean waters, conserve and recover vulnerable marine wildlife, protect ocean ecosystems, and establish ocean wilderness. The conservancy publishes *Blue Planet Quarterly* and the annual *Health of the Oceans* report. Current issues of these publications are available on its website as are fact sheets, the quarterly newsletter *Coastal Connection*, and other reports such as *Cruise Control: How Cruise Ships Affect the Marine Environment.*

SeaWeb
1731 Connecticut Ave. NW, 4th Floor, Washington, DC 20009
(202) 483-9570
e-mail: seaweb@seaweb.org • website: www. seaweb.org

SeaWeb is a multimedia educational project established by the Pew Charitable Trusts with the mission to raise awareness of the ocean and issues related to its conservation. SeaWeb publishes reports such as *Danger at Sea: Our Changing Oceans* and *The Ocean Report* as well as the monthly newsletter *Ocean Update*, all of which are available on its website.

Whale and Dolphin Conservation Society (WDCS)
Brookfield House
38 St. Paul St., Chippenham, Wiltshire, UK SN15 1LY
(44) (0)1249 449500 • fax: (44) (0)1249 449501
e-mail: info@wdcs.org • website: www.wdcs.org

WDCS is dedicated to the conservation and welfare of all whales, dolphins and porpoises (also known as cetaceans). The society's objectives are to reduce and ultimately eliminate the continuing threats to cetaceans and their habitats and to raise awareness of cetaceans and educate people about the need to address the continuing threats to their welfare and survival. WDCS publishes papers, reports and other literature on a variety of topics relating to whales and dolphins and *WDCS Magazine*, selections of which are available on its website.

World Wildlife Fund (WWF-US)
1250 24th St. NW, Washington, DC 20037-1193
(202) 293-4800 • fax: (202) 293-9211
e-mail: PIResponse@wwfus.org • website: www.worldwildlife.org

WWF is a global organization acting locally through a network of family offices. The largest privately supported international conservation organization, WWF is dedicated to protecting the world's wildlife and wildlands. WWF directs its conservation efforts toward protecting endangered spaces, saving endangered species, and addressing global threats. WWF-US publishes reports such as *The Fishery Effects of Marine Reserves and Fishery Closures* and *Trawling in the Mist* and other ocean conservation resources on its website.

Bibliography of Books

Terry L. Anderson and Henry I. Miller, eds. *The Greening of U.S. Foreign Policy*. Stanford, CA: Hoover Institution Press, 2000.

Ronald Bailey, ed. *Earth Report 2000: Revisiting the True State of the Planet*. New York: McGraw-Hill, 2000.

Dana Beach *Coastal Sprawl: The Effects of Urban Design on Aquatic Ecosystems in the United States*. Arlington, VA: Pew Oceans Commission, 2002.

Michael Brower and Warren Leon *The Consumer's Guide to Effective Environmental Choices: Practical Advice from the Union of Concerned Scientists*. New York: Three Rivers Press, 1999.

John R. Clark *Coastal Seas: The Conservation Challenge*. Malden, MA: Blackwell Science, 1998.

J. Pat Dowdy *Coastal Conservation and Management: An Ecological Perspective*. Boston: Kluwer Academic Publishers, 2001.

Frances Drake *Global Warming: The Science of Climate Change*. London: Oxford University Press, 2000.

Robert L. Friedheim, ed. *Toward a Sustainable Whaling Regime*. Edmonton: Canadian Circumpolar Institute Press, 2001.

Rebecca J. Goldburg, Matthew S. Elliot, and Rosamond L. Naylor *Marine Aquaculture in the United States: Environmental Impacts and Policy Options*. Arlington, VA: Pew Oceans Commission, 2001.

Mark Hertsgaard *Earth Odyssey: Around the World in Search of Our Environmental Future*. New York: Broadway Books, 1998.

Don Hinrichsen *Coastal Waters of the World: Trends, Threats, and Strategies*. Washington, DC: Island Press, 1998.

Gregor Hodgson and Jennifer Liebeler *The Global Coral Reef Crisis: Trends and Solutions*. Los Angeles: Reef Check Foundation, 2002.

Independent World Commission on the Oceans *The Ocean, Our Future*. New York: Cambridge University Press, 1998.

Nihon-Kujirarui Kenky ujo *Whaling Controversy and the Rational Utilization of Marine Resources*. Tokyo: Institute of Cetacean Research, 2002.

Robert W. Knecht and Biliana Cicin-Sain *The Future of U.S. Ocean Policy: Choices for a New Century*. Washington, DC: Island Press, 1998.

Bjorn Lomborg *The Skeptical Environmentalist: Measuring the Real State of the World*. London: Cambridge University Press, 2001.

Kenneth Henry Mann	*Ecology of Coastal Waters: With Implications for Management.* Malden, MA: Blackwell Science, 2000.
Sue Mayer	*A Review of the Scientific Justifications for Maintaining Cetaceans in Captivity: A Report for the Whale and Dolphin Conservation Society (WDCS).* Bath, UK: WDCS, 1998.
William McCloskey	*Their Fathers' Work: Casting Nets with the World's Fishermen.* New York: McGraw-Hill, 1998.
Patrick J. Michaels and Robert C. Balling Jr.	*The Satanic Gases: Clearing the Air About Global Warming.* Washington, DC: Cato Institute, 2000.
Thomas Gale Moore	*Climate of Fear: Why We Shouldn't Worry About Global Warming.* Washington, DC: Cato Institute, 1998.
Edward Moran	*The Global Ecology.* New York: H.W. Wilson, 1999.
Kieran Mulvaney	*The Whaling Season: An Inside Account of the Struggle to Stop Commercial Whaling.* Washington, DC: Island Press/Shearwater Books, 2003.
Richard O'Barry	*To Free a Dolphin.* Los Angeles: Renaissance Books, 2000.
Daniel Pauly and Jay Maclean	*In a Perfect Ocean: The States of Fisheries and Ecosystems in the North Atlantic Ocean.* Washington, DC: Island Press, 2003.
S. George Philander	*Is the Temperature Rising? The Uncertain Science of Global Warming.* Princeton, NJ: Princeton University Press, 1998.
Ellen J. Prager	*The Ocean.* New York: McGraw-Hill, 2000.
Carl Safina	*Song for the Blue Ocean: Encounters Along the World's Coasts and Beneath the Seas.* New York: Henry Holt, 1998.
Carl Safina	*Eye of the Albatross: Visions of Hope and Survival.* New York: Henry Holt, 2002.
Philip M. Scanlon	*The Dolphins Are Back: A Successful Quality Model for Healing the Environment.* Portland, OR: Productivity Press, 1998.
F. John Vernberg	*The Coastal Zone: Past, Present, and Future.* Columbia: University of South Carolina Press, 2001.
Colin Woodard	*Ocean's End: Travels Through Endangered Seas.* New York: Basic Books, 2000.

Index